Redemption
Through The Blood

Teen Challenge reaching out
to Scotland's drug problem

by Paul Flynn

Xulon PRESS

Copyright © 2016 by Paul flynn

Redemption through the blood
Teen Challenge reaching out to Scotland's drug problem
by Paul flynn

Printed in the United States of America.

ISBN 9781498485425

All rights reserved solely by the author. The author guarantees all contents are original and do not infringe upon the legal rights of any other person or work. No part of this book may be reproduced in any form without the permission of the author. The views expressed in this book are not necessarily those of the publisher.

Unless otherwise indicated,Scripture quotations taken from the Holy Bible New International Version NIV copyright 1973, 1978, 1984, 2011 by Biblica Inc. TM used by permission of Zondervan. All rights reserved worldwide. www.zondervan.com Published jointly by Tyndale House Publishers, Inc. And Zondervan. 2005

www.xulonpress.com

DISCLAIMER

Please note that the names of some people mentioned in this book have been changed to protect their privacy.

INTRODUCTION

I have written this as spoken in Scottish dialect and grammar. There are explanations with most of these colloquial sayings and my intention is to reach out to the sick, hurting and give guidance for Christians to realize how great God's grace is for everyone.

My purpose in writing this book is to expose the disastrous consequences of not living life God's way, but more importantly that no one is beyond the reach of God's love. Like all of us, I am still a work in progress. My experience as a Christian has been meeting so many Christians who have put laws to God's grace, and I'm hoping that this book can teach people to let go and let God.

My drug and alcohol addictions started at the age of thirteen and continued full on for ten years.

Reading my story, it might seem as if I have dropped back into addictions of one kind or another many times. To put it into perspective, the twelve-year period of being clean and sober had in total less than four months of addiction to drugs and alcohol. So you can read the amazing changes Jesus has made in my life from a damaged life to a life of purpose.

THE FIRST SEVEN YEARS

If you asked me about sin, I would have to say that as far back as I can remember, I was always good at making wrong choices.

I grew up in Bonnie Scotland, in the small town of Coatbridge, just outside Glasgow. My Dad, Mum, two big sisters and I lived in a three-up block of flats in an area called Sikeside. For those who don't know what a three-up is, it's a building with a ground floor and two other floors above.

My Mum's twin sister, Jean lived in the same block as us, with her two sons and her daughter. My Dad felt responsible for looking after her and her kids. They had quite a troubled life, but there was love in their family. Once my cousin left the chip pan on and fell asleep, and my Dad had to go up and put out the fire. At times, my Dad had to sort out the trouble going on in the house between my aunt and her ex-partner. This was mainly through alcohol and violence.

The home I grew up in, just below my Aunt Jean in the same block of flats, was a lot less trouble. Don't get me wrong — now and then my Gran visited for a drink and would come down from my Aunt Jean's screaming drunk, and start kicking our door. My Dad didn't like my Gran drinking in front of us when we were kids. I remember at Christmas or New Year time, it was my Gran who always started the fights in her house. You see, she was an alcoholic and a chain smoker. She passed away when I was thirteen. I remember her in her wheelchair, as her legs had been cut off as a result of excessive alcohol and chain smoking. I can mind (remember) when my Mum told me Gran passed away and I felt the grief of her death. Even though I have seen with my own eyes what drink and smoking had done to my Gran, it clearly didn't scare me. Her death didn't teach me not to drink and smoke.

When I was six, my older sister was in her early teens. I knew she had a boyfriend and was smoking. I would say that I'd tell Dad she smoked if she didn't take me to my other cousins at the far end of Coatbridge, so I could play with them. Blackmailing as a kid! I suppose I knew since I was the youngest and the only boy at this time, I could get away with it.

Around six years old, I began to steal money out of the house to buy sweets at the ice cream van. My best mate at that time was Tosh. We didn't live that far from each other. Tosh's older brother, Paddy, was best mates with my older cousin, Gordon at that time. I still remember the day I was in my parents' room and I had seen money on their kitchen unit. It was there to pay the bills. I decided to take one of the £20 notes, hoping they wouldn't realize, but as if!! I was standing at the ice cream van outside Paddy and Tosh's flat, planning to buy everyone sweeties at the van, when I heard one of my Mum's friends shouting me up, knowing that my Mum was looking for the money but not knowing where it had gone to. I can remember my Mum taking me back home when she got the money. My Dad was standing on the verandah, not too happy with me. I only had to look at my Dad and straight away I knew he wasn't happy with me. You only had to look at my Dad's eyes and that said enough.

Another time I was with my friend, Tosh in his home and I was thinking how to get into the kitchen and take money out of his Mum's purse, so I asked his Mum if I could go into the kitchen to get a drink. In the kitchen I noticed the purse, looked in it and stole a £5 note. Then Tosh and I left the house and went out. Tosh knew nothing about what I'd done. Secretly I dropped the note on the ground, bent down to pick it up and showed Tosh what I had "found." We were both so excited and couldn't wait to get to the ice cream van to buy sweeties. While we were waiting on the ice cream van to show up, we were playing soccer with one of our mates and his Dad. All of a sudden, my cousin Gordon and Tosh's older brother, Paddy ran up, asking where the £5 was. Tosh was shouting that it was mine and that he'd been there when I'd found it. I'm sure when Tosh 's M um opened her purse and it was empty, she realized it was me that took the money. Who else was in the kitchen? It had to be me. It was pointless saying I found it, I'm sure they know where it had come from. Theft and trouble was something I was going to have to get used to.

I remember another time in Sikeside. I ran about with a boy a year younger than me. He came up to me, saying he knew where some needles were. He took me to a flat behind the flat I lived in. We went into the Dumpster and went into the trash. He showed me the needles for drugs and I took a needle off him and was playing with it. I was only six, but I knew it was for some kind of drug. My Dad had noticed us and saw what we were doing. I remember the shock on his face as he shouted out of the window and then came down and took it off me.

There were loads of shut-down factories in my town. Once it had been known for having a lot of steel works. So many Irish came to

Coatbridge to work at one time that some people today call it Little Ireland, and many people there have Irish blood. The Prime Minister at that time in the 80s was Maggie Thatcher. Her name is like a bad word in Scotland, as she had a reputation for closing down the factories. Much of the middle class was really struggling at that time all over Scotland and other parts of the UK.

I remember that there was serious trouble in Northern Ireland back then, and even some bombing by the I.R.A. in England. The paramilitary groups were at war with each other, and the Protestant vs. Catholic conflict was always on the news. Because I was a Catholic, along with most of the people I ran about with, and we supported Celtic, a soccer team from a city in Scotland called Glasgow, I suppose my thinking was that I should believe in the I.R.A. In a sense, many young kids I knew believed that was the way to go. We were young and vulnerable. It was like, "I'm a Catholic and I support Celtic, so we are going to be against the Protestants who support Rangers," another soccer team from Glasgow. This was the West of Scotland mentality. Following the group, that was me.

As a kid, my Dad was Catholic and my Mum was Protestant. Many people in West Scotland have got Scottish and Irish blood. When I wrote about having the same blood, I meant your second name can mean a lot to us because Irish second name usually means you're a Catholic, and British second name usually means Protestant. And that's what I mean about Irish or British blood. The culture can be very small-minded on religion and judging people for having different religion.

My Dad used to take me and my older sisters to a Catholic chapel. We honestly hated it. I don't know about my sisters, but I didn't really listen to any of it, though I did get a feeling of God's spirit being there. Another question I had with the Bible and God being real was that I was told we all came from apes. You see, when you're a kid, you seem to believe lies a lot easier, especially if adults tell you those lies. I can remember in the chapel in Sikeside, tearing up the hymn book because I was angry about having to get up and sing, especially when I really didn't want to be there.

I had an attraction to the wrong things when I was growing up, like the gang in the neighborhood I was from — the Y-D, the Young Dykes. You see, Sikeside and Greenend were the worst places to live in Coatbridge. Most people saw Sikeside and Greenend as one place because they joined together, and those who lived there in a sense saw it as the same place, even though Greenend was built before Sikeside. All the young ones from Sikeside and Greenend, including me, used to go to a path and throw stones at the other kids in Carnbroe. Carnbroe was quite a posh place in Coatbridge, and those of us in Greenend and Sikeside were a lot more rough and ready. At a path there was a big dip down near the path we used to fight on before going up to Carnbroe, and youngsters would throw stones back at us. It was kids trying to fit into a gang from Sikeside and Greenend and also the Carnbroe kids doing the same. I can recall during it I would go the furthest down the hill towards the Carnbroe kids. It was a little period of conflict between us kids. I was probably the youngest there, but I've always pushed the boundaries.

The primary school I went to was called St. Stephen's Primary Catholic School, and the property joined up with a Protestant school called Sikeside Primary. This was in the 80s, when there was a lot of war between the Catholics and Protestants, and trouble spread to parts of England and the west of Scotland. You see, we had the same sort of problem too. One half supported the Catholic armed groups and the other half supported the Protestant armed groups. As kids, many of us went along with it, and the students in the primary I went to would shout through the fence to the Protestant kids, "Protestant dogs eat the frogs in a Sunday morning," and the Protestant kids would shout, "Catholic cats eat the rats in a Sunday morning." You see, even as kids, we were brought up to think our religion was right and better than theirs.

Even football got brought into it; Celtic F.C. was a Catholic team and the Rangers were a Protestant team, and a lot of grown-ups on the two sides hated each other, and I really mean hated each other. Everything you could think of or any excuse you could find to hate the other side, you would try to find fault. Politics got brought into religion as well. "If you love Ireland, go back there then, Catholic side." The British government has got a lot to answer for. A lot of Catholics would bring up the past when Britain ruled a lot of countries, and Catholics would see it as bullying other countries. I mean, bringing things up from many years ago. The two sides would always talk about past wars. To be honest, those of us in Scotland who had bitterness in them about politics and war in Northern Ireland didn't really know exactly what was going on in Northern Ireland. The only ones who understood it were those who were there, living among all the troubles. Most of us had never even been there. We were only hearing what we wanted to hear.

It wasn't all bad. I remember having a sense of security then. I was loved by my family. I was always looked after. I also had my two big cousins around, and because of that I didn't feel as much fear. I always knew the love of my parents and my two big sisters. I believe all kids should feel that family unity.

ALBION STREET

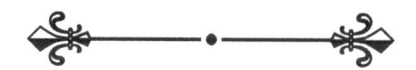

I was seven years of age and my Dad and Mum were planning to move to a place in Coatbridge called Albion Street, about a half hour walk from Sikeside. At seven, you see, it was a good distance. I knew one lad the same age as me who lived there. His dad knew my family. My Dad's brother, his wife and my two younger cousins didn't live that far from us. My uncle was what you would call in Scotland and Ireland a rebel; he loved Celtic F.C. and saw himself as Irish instead of Scottish. You see, their dad, my Grandad, was from Ireland so they were 100 percent Irish blood. [Explanation — when you use Mom and Dad as NAMES, they're capitalized, but when you use mom and dad talking about someone else's parents, they're lowercased.]

It wasn't long after we got there that my Aunty Jean met a man named Sean, who was born in Ireland and had moved to Scotland with his parents, settling in Coatbridge. My Mum and Aunty Jean were out one night in an area called Coatdyke, not far from where we lived. My Mum and aunty were standing in Coatdyke and this big silver car was flashing its lights at them. They were wondering who this guy was in the car like a successful businessman would own. They went into the pub, Mum and Aunty Jean, with Sean carrying a briefcase as businessmen usually do. You see, Sean knew my Aunty Jean's ex man. Mad Pat, we called him. Sean got to know my Aunty Jean through Mad Pat. My Aunty Jean took a bit of a dislike to this man, Sean. She thought he saw himself as better than they were, the way he went about as a successful business man and anyway, why would a big-time businessman have any interest in her? Sean had noticed Jean and took an interest. Jean was shocked. She couldn't believe it. Not long after that, they got to know each other and they decided that they liked each other. Mind, the home was a bit mad at times! My Aunt Jean was thinking she'd hit the jackpot, no turning back now for Aunty Jean, she'd made it. Well, so she thought. Away to live a new life in sunny Kilsyth. Saying "sunny" is a Scottish way of being humorous in a sarcastic way, because Kilsyth is an ordinary place.

Sean had met my Aunty Jean in a nightclub (Barnyard) not long before he noticed her with my Mum in Coatdyke. Sean had been flashing his car lights to get Jean's attention. It wasn't long before Aunty Jean and her two youngest kids moved to Sean's place at Kilsyth, where he had a fancy home. My Aunty Jean had seen what Sean had there and was thinking she'd hit the jackpot — a businessman with a big, fancy car and a lovely home. But why was a man like that paying any interest in her? She came from a three-up flat in Sikeside with three kids.

Her oldest son didn't move in with them because he had decided to join the army, and a year later he came to live with my Mum and us. As I said before, we had a home in Albion Street, and by this time, my Dad and Mum decided to split up. I can still remember the day I found out. I was in Sikeside playing outside Tosh's flat, and my Mum came to pick me up. She had been crying. I didn't really take it that bad that they had split up. My parents grew apart as time went on. I'm not sure why it didn't hurt me that much at that time. I mean, at seven I honestly didn't even see them going apart.

I had started a new primary school, St. Patrick's Primary. I suppose in some areas it was different from the one in Sikeside, St. Stephen's Primary. Without being judgmental in any way, it seemed that the kids there had come from families where there was less stress, and there was less unemployment. The kids in Sikeside did have love in their homes, but a lot of us had also seen a lot of madness.

It didn't take long before I began to feel out of place in my new school. I was in the bottom group, for a start, because the rest of the kids were more educated than me. Don't get me wrong, that wasn't the whole reason. The teacher could be teaching the class and I wouldn't listen to one thing she was teaching. I could sit from nine till three and hardly write any work, and not even listen, either. Writing and reading I could do, no problem, even though I hardly ever did it.

There were only a few of us on a free dinner ticket, which means the children living with unemployed parents got a ticket for free dinner, and I honestly hated getting called up by the teacher to go to the front of the class to get it. It was like a punishment. I can still remember once not getting up to get it. I felt out of place partly because I was thinking that other kids there were better than I was, because their parents were doing fine financially and they always looked as though they had a better life than me, plus they were more educated.

Despite not feeling like I fit in, I did make new friends in my class, and there were also some kids from my class who lived near me. We did the usual things kids do, play football and other games. I didn't see that much trouble. I didn't see much crime in Albion Street, compared to Sikeside. To be honest, I still got myself into trouble a lot, with theft and being cheeky.

At this time, my Dad met a woman named Patricia, from a village called Harthill. I had never heard of it before. After that, my schedule was like Monday to Friday at Mum's, then Friday to Monday at Harthill. My two sisters also used to go visit my Dad in Harthill, but not as much as me. On Monday morning, I would get a bus to St. Patrick's Primary, which was near St. Patrick's High School. Teenagers from Harthill direction would get on that bus to go to school. It was one bus going to the Catholic school. You see, Harthill and the other villages near there were mainly Protestant. That area had a reputation for being bitter Protestant — I'm sure not everyone there was, but there was quite a majority.

When my Dad met Patricia, I was seven on the verge of turning eight. I can recall seeing the Orange walks (Protestants) and also the Hibs walks (Catholics). The walks were like wars that happened in the past, showing that they were proud of their religion. My Dad sometimes carried the banner for the Hibs. Till this day, I still don't know the exact reason for them. Talk about feeling out of place! There I was, a young Catholic, second name Flynn which is Irish, supporting Celtic, and from a town that was known for having a lot of Catholics in it. Not just that, but there was a major war going on between Catholics, Protestants, and the British Army. My soccer team at that time wasn't doing so good compared to the Rangers, and where I'm from, that was a big thing.

There was a small chapel in Harthill. It was quite busy and was used by the Catholics who were from that way. My Dad and his girlfriend used to take me and her daughters to it. Again, I didn't want to go. You see, my Dad's girlfriend happened to be a Catholic. We used to go, and even though I didn't want to be there, on the way out I felt like some kind of clean spirit, as if God was there.

In Harthill, they took the walks really seriously. They would have their flags hanging just outside their windows. The colors told the stories — Protestant was red, white and blue, Catholic was green, white and gold. You see, that was the color of your identity. If you were wearing green, white and gold in an area that was Protestant, you would stick out, and vice versa. On the street where my Dad lived, I got friendly with two brothers who happened to be big Rangers fans. At the start, I felt really accepted, but after a while that changed because they grew up taking a dislike to Catholics.

Funny too, because during the week back in Coatbridge at my Mum's, I ran about with Catholics, so I became a mixed-up kid through this religion.

In Coatbridge, I lived near a kid my age. We used to go to the public swimming pool, and afterwards I decided to go and steal toys out of shops, so we did. It was like I was getting all those toys for free. I can even remember his mum had some money left out to pay someone, and I felt like taking a pound coin, but I got found out and she told my Mum. I was so frightened about it. There was a road just down from her house, and to get attention, I walked out in front of a car. The car swerved out of the way and the driver looked at me as if to say, "What is that kid doing?" I can't remember telling anyone about that, but that was how far I would go to get myself out of the problem I had got myself into. You see, I know it was only a pound coin but it was the principle of stealing out of someone's home again.

I recall that I was with a young lad in Albion Street, and he was telling me his big brother smoked cannabis. I told him that I believed that was wrong and he believed it wasn't that bad. I was about ten at that time, 1989–1990. The music scene was changing and a drug called ecstasy was getting very popular. I was aware that the older ones took it.

Back in Harthill, my Dad and his new family (Patricia and her three daughters) were getting along great. There was plenty of love in the home. Patricia was a very loving and caring woman, seeing me and my two big sisters as her own. They did all they could to make sure we came first, and we were never without. It wasn't as if there was plenty of money, but we didn't really struggle for anything.

As a kid, I always had to be around friends. I hated just sitting in the house and would always rather be out and about with the kids in Coatbridge or Harthill, either area. I was a really outgoing kid and always had to be out doing stuff. I suppose I really felt out of place in Harthill and never accepted by others. You see, the ones I ran about with were a year or more older than me, Rangers fans, and a bit bitter towards Catholics. Don't get me wrong, some were worse than others, and they never hurt me, but it was more what they said about Catholics or Celtic supporters. They weren't terrible kids. I believe they got all this stuff spoken into them as kids too. I always felt different to them. I also grew up pretty bitter towards Protestants, just like them, but I always believed they were worse and they thought we were worse.

My friend Mick, in Albion Street, had three brothers and two sisters. One of his older brothers was going the wrong way. My friend was the youngest in the house. I think I got him into a bit of trouble in school as well as out of school. In Primary 7, we had too many pupils in our class, so some of the youngest went into another class. He enjoyed it in the smaller class and his work really improved. As for me, I still didn't listen to what the teacher was teaching, as I had no real interest in learning.

At the end of Primary 7, I was eleven years old and my Mum told me and my sisters that we were moving back to Sikeside, but to a different, quieter area. She had put in an advertisement for a house exchange and another family saw it and wanted to swap. Just at that time, my Mum met a man who lived just across from us in Albion Street. His name was John, and he and my Mum started getting to know each other. But as she wasn't that happy in Albion Street, she decided to accept the swap and move to Sikeside. Going into first year of high school and going back to where I was born, Sikeside didn't know what to expect.

When I moved back to Sikeside, a lot of the flats had been knocked down. When we got there, I already knew some people, but my Mum preferred me hanging around with the kids in Dalvien, a different part of Sikeside. I did know them, but not that well. At the beginning, I was running around Dalvien and going to some of the guys' homes, playing Playstation or soccer. Again, I felt out of place with them. I can remember walking through the Ash path that leads to Cumbrae Crescent in Sikeside where I was born, and I met my old friend Tosh, standing on the stairs with a few guys. He told me he had found out who was in his class at high school and that I was in all his classes and our group was 1.4E. Imagine, my old mate and me in the same group through high school! Another time I met Tosh he was with a guy, Gurie, I knew from St. Stephen's Primary. I can remember fighting him and pulling out his hair. I had a fistful of blonde hair in my hand. But this time when I saw him, he had grown in size.

I started running about Cumbrae again with Tosh and another mate I had known called Mark. Another guy they knew was a year older and a lot taller. Little did I know that he was the bully there. When I was down in Cumbrae after my Aunty Jean and my cousins had moved away, I felt pretty lonely then. They were all smoking and I had never really thought of smoking. It was a late night in Cumbrae Crescent and the guys I was with were smoking dope. I was surprised at that, but to them it was no big deal. It didn't take me long before I wanted to smoke it. The first thing I had to do was learn to inhale, so I used to steal my Mum's cigarettes and go away and try to inhale the smoke. I just couldn't do it.

One night, another guy from Cumbrae and I decided to buy cigarettes. He was two or three years older than me, so he was already smoking, and that night I actually learned to inhale. I was so proud of myself, but I had to get rid of the smell of the smoke before I got home. I was twelve years old, and now that I had learned to smoke, I could try dope. Couldn't wait!

Tosh's older brother, Paddy got involved in drug dealing at this time. He looked like the happiest guy you could meet, loving life. Plenty of drugs, never short of money, going to all the biggest raves in Scotland, and popular with a lot of the women in Coatbridge and Airdrie. His life looked very attractive, and the kind of life you would think everyone in our area would want. Life couldn't get any better.

Paddy, Tosh and their two sisters and younger brother were brought up in a home where their father and mother were Catholics. Their dad, Pat, liked a drink, their wee mum, Liz, was what you would call a little housewife. She had faith and she always made sure her kids were safe from any harm out in the streets. But when Liz's children left school and moved on, Liz couldn't stop them from making their own choices in life. Paddy and Tosh loved it when their dad came back from the pub and told them the stories. Stories of their dad's drinking nights out and all the laughs he had.

Pat and Liz had put structure in their kids, but kids down our way hated that. We all wanted to do our own thing. We used to make fun of each other if our parents told us to come home early. Truth is, our parents were no doubt worried about us. It was so easy for any one of us to go down the wrong path. Nearly all of us who ran about with each other were brought up as Catholics, so we all got some awareness of who Jesus was. If it wasn't in chapel, then it was at school, but I don't think any of us cared or even spoke about Jesus. I could just imagine all of us in our early teens talking about the Lord. Our goal was everything but.

ST. PATRICK'S HIGH SCHOOL

The best thing about starting high school was knowing Tosh and I were going to be in the same class. The two of us could read each other's minds on this, and that meant we were going to be trouble in the classroom. We were already running about with each other. We went through school, and the classes we liked depended on what the teacher was like. I didn't care about education or passing exams and then going to find a job. At that age, the only thing on our minds was what you would call doing nothing but pleasing the flesh. If you spoke to us about clean spirits, we would have thought you were talking about alcohol. I mean, I don't know about Tosh, but Jesus to me then was a Catholic. My thinking then was that I'd get to heaven because I was a Catholic and I'd been to chapel, Catholic church. It was like that was my pass into heaven. I can't remember anyone telling me that you had to be born again.

The first year passed, and I'm sure I could have done better, but I chose not to. Second year came, and a lot changed for the worse. By thirteen, I was introduced to some drugs. After school we would either sit in the entrance hall of one of the closes (inside the block of flats) or on a small wall outside the flats. We were all smoking cannabis. Near the wall where we all hung around, there was a dealer in that flat, and that was one of the places where we got our cannabis.

There was a man who lived on the ground floor of one of the flats; we called him Jackie Munchkin. You didn't see much of Jackie, he was a grown man. People in our area knew about this man and that he had a reputation for sexually abusing kids. That's no doubt why he never left his home, because people knew about him. One night, he asked us to get him a bit of cannabis, so we got him what he wanted. We all knew he had a reputation for being called a beast, but most of us didn't know much about it, apart from Matt, who lived in Sikeside. Jackie was said to have done something sexual to my mate's younger cousins, but all that time no one ever spoke about it, as Jackie said he would ask us to get out of his flat if we brought it up in a conversation. He wasn't reported because the kids were scared of him. We didn't really know all this at the time. All we wanted was a smoke in his flat, somewhere to sit out of the cold.

Sometimes Jackie would get a smoke with us, but he didn't let us in his home at this point. We just sat beneath his ground floor window. After a while, he let us in. Matt's mum was not supposed to know that Matt was in Jackie's home. I suppose Jackie was taking a risk here. One weekend, a mate and I were planning to go halves buying L.S.D., so we met a Sikeside guy called Big James, who was selling it. The acid we bought was called a strawberry. I knew James' younger brother because we were the same age. The two of us went back to Jackie's home with the acid and cut it in two. I honestly loved the feeling of it. It was like we were all great friends and we all loved each other.

I had a problem then. It was my grandad's birthday and all my Mum's family were there. The party was in my Mum's house. I can still remember going home, high on drugs with this half a strawberry (L.S.D.). When I got home, everyone was happy and drunk at my Grandad Ewart's party. I couldn't go in the living room to say, "Hi," to them all, as I was freaking out. I had to go upstairs where my oldest cousin, Mark and my sister were, and I felt a bit more safe. They didn't realize I was tripping.

One of the people we ran around with at that time was one year older than us and a good bit taller. He was a bit of a bully to most of us, except Mark. Mark's family was the largest family. What I mean by "largest" was that they were a family you would not mess with because there were many of them, and some were known for violence and crime, down our way. Plus he had two big brothers who weren't scared of him. Mark also had a big cousin who had the reputation for being the best fighter in the Y-D for his age group. A lot of us looked up to the these guys in the Y-D, most of them being about five years older than we were, and we wanted to be like them when we grew up. They were the ones we got our drugs from. There was a small rave (music and drugs) near our way and the Y-D ruled it. Everyone would talk about their violence. At one point, the bouncers would let them in first if they would stop fighting, but that didn't happen.

The next step into the world of drugs was that I got introduced to speed, and I took a half gram of it in Jackie's home. Again, I loved the feeling of escaping, though I didn't understand that at thirteen. In Jackie's home there was a small entrance hall with a second door leading into the living room, and one guy called this wee room the digger. He would choose one of us to go into the digger, and give us a few punches and kicks. It was like we didn't have the choice to say no, because the one doing the punches was a lot stronger and taller, though he never chose Mark. Jackie must have enjoyed this, as he had a hatred for youngsters. I can't remember any of us being able to talk about it, as he would have thrown us out of his flat. Like I said, Jackie got away with it because the kids didn't turn up at court through fear.

The younger brother of Big James (who I got the acid from) had done something to Jackie and Jackie was said to have put his hands round James' brother's neck. Not long after that, we were in Jackie's home playing my Playstation when the door opened and all the Y-D were at the door. Someone said something cheeky to Jackie, then all of a sudden Big James jumps in the house and starts attacking Jackie. Then others joined in kicking him. Not long after that, Jackie decided to move home. I remember I had £5, and I had to decide to either get a £5 bit of cannabis or else buy Jackie a picture with a wee dolphin in it. I bought the gift thinking I was doing the right thing saying goodbye. My thinking then was that he would be thankful for it. I chose to buy Jackie the picture instead of the dope. I went to his door and handed him the photo. He took it, but gave me a right dirty look.

There is one more thing I remember that happened at Jackie's before he moved away. We met a teenage girl who had moved down to Sikeside from Airdrie. She was about our age. She had two friends from Airdrie with her one evening, and we all ended up in Jackie's home. Liam asked this blonde if I could kiss her, and she agreed, so we went out to the wee room between the living room and the front door. This was my first real kiss. We were kissing, I was terrified, my legs shaking, both our faces covered in saliva. I didn't know when to stop, until someone came to the front door. That was IT. After that, I thought I was in love.

The problem was that we lived in different towns, the girl Liam was seeing, her friend, and the one I liked, or should I say the one I was obsessed with after one kiss! Matt and I would get the train to Airdrie to see them, but the one I liked had started going out with a young guy from that area. But I thought I loved her. Do you know, once I ran away and was planning to sleep in Liams' girlfriend's back garden, just to be close to her. But Liam's' girlfriend's mother said I could stay in their house for one night.

When Matt and I were running round, there we were at the train station and decided to set the fire extinguisher off on the train. So the police came to get me. It was my first time getting arrested by the police. I was thirteen. The police took me back to my Mum's and they were surprised that where I was living was a house, not a flat.

I can remember when I moved back to Sikeside and we were all speaking about something and I used the word 'police.' Everyone started laughing, because they didn't use that word, and they said, 'It's the screws.'

I can still remember in Albion Street deciding to go to a Catholic chapel called All Saints. Now back then, no one told me to go. You see, my Mum was brought up a Protestant, so the only time I went to Catholic chapel was with the primary school. When I was in my early teens, submitting my life to God was totally alien to me. I loved sin, and everything about the flesh got me going. I didn't know much about surrendering my life to God. I thought that was all dark and old religious nonsense.

We had just moved back to Sikeside when my Mum told us she was pregnant. I was so surprised; I thought I was always going to be the youngest in the family. My Mum had another son, Nicholas, when I was twelve, and I was jealous to start with. Up till then I had got most of the attention, as I had been the youngest, and I was also the only boy. I first met Nicholas when he was just born, and all those jealous feelings left me. I was left looking at my wee brother. From then on and while he grew up, I was very protective of him.

SECOND YEAR

Through the second year at St. Patrick's High, Tosh and I had something that made us proud. Our class, 2.4E, was the worst class in our year, and the worst three were me, Tosh, and a girl we called Taz. It got to the stage where getting suspended was something we got used to.

A few of us were at the Ash parks where football teams would meet to play each other. A few of us noticed two young guys we didn't recognize. They were our age, but one was wearing a Scotland tracksuit and he had a middle shed (center parting). We followed the two of them to Arran Avenue and started giving them cheek. The guy in the tracksuit shouted up to the flat he had just moved into with his mum. His big sister, Donna came to the verandah. The guy then said, if any of us had a problem, we should come on the grass and fight it out. He was standing there, offering any of us a square go, but none of us had the bottle. None of us went on the grass to fight him. We were the ones who looked like the idiots. His nickname was Jazza.

You know, when we were all running around together, we weren't allowed to be different. If we spoke in a different way, wore different clothes or even listen to different music, we would get the confidence taken of us, like our mates would make fun of us. If we were all sitting about and someone new came into our area, we would all talk about that person and see if we could find any faults in them, and then all make fun of them. It was like trying to find other people's weak spots. Jazza ended up hanging around with guys a few years older than us, getting into acid, 'E' and other drugs. Before we knew it, he was hanging around with us.

My Dad had moved from Harthill back to Sikeside because my Mum had got in touch with him, saying she needed help with the way I was living. So Dad got a one-bedroom flat in Cumbrae Crescent. You see, I had stopped going to Harthill and just ran about Coatbridge. Dad still went back to Harthill to see his woman, Patricia. Drugs had become my god at the age of thirteen, but I hadn't realized it. Everything I wanted to grow up like was actually taking place. My friends were my family now. I always said at that age that I wished I had a dad who dealt drugs and had done jail before, but instead I had a Dad who loved and cared for his children. It wasn't just that there weren't many men who would stand on my Dad's toes because he knew how to fight. He had never been in gangs or got into trouble with the police. He just looked after the ones he loved. But at my age, I just didn't see it.

THIRD YEAR, AGE FOURTEEN

My Dad had asked me if I wanted to go to a different high school, and I decided to go to Calder Head High School in Shotts, not that far from Harthill. I remember my first day at this high school. I walked into a class and decided to light up a cigarette. so I did. The other kids in the class couldn't believe it. Guess what — I was suspended on my first day at Calder Head High. So much for me getting my head screwed on.

I remember there was a lad in my class, who I had seen with L.S.D. So what did I do? I asked him if he could give me one and I would give him the money another time, and surprisingly he agreed. This was when we were getting our shorts and T-shirts on for P.E., ready for playing basketball. I started tripping while trying to play, freaking out. The P.E. teacher was there. I was running all over the place, hallucinating, while this orange ball was flying about. After the lesson I got dressed and missed the other classes, as I was still freaking out.

I was only at that school for a few months. One day I said something about one of the guys there, he and his mates threatened me, and I just left the school, jumped on a bus and headed back to Coatbridge.

There was a lot of good in me despite all the wrong decisions I made growing up. I got a bit mixed up about life. The right way for me to go was a boring, long and pointless journey. I wanted things fast. When I grew up, I always heard at school everyone speaking about the gang members. Not many of us had role models, so that's why we saw these gang members as people we respected from my area. A lot of us looked up to these guys; they were our role models. You see, most of us had parents who had split up.

If any of my uncles and aunts or grandparents from my Dad's side came into the house and I was there at the time, I wouldn't say a word to them except yes or no. I felt I had no interest in them, and I didn't believe they had any interest in me. As I said before, my friends were my family now. I hated being outside with my biological family. The only time I really paid any attention to them was when I wanted something. I could never just sit in the house with them. I always had to be out in the streets.

St. Patrick's High School took me back when I left Calder Head in Shotts. Back in Sikeside, I ran with the same guys as before, except Jazza was hanging around with us. I remember when he came round to my Dad's house in Sikeside, the one-bedroom flat. The two of us got on very well.

When I got back to Sikeside after a few months away in Harthill, a couple in their early twenties was living there. I knew one of them, Lynn. She was with Gary, a guy from Glasgow. They were into a drug called KIT. I had never heard of this drug before, so I decided to find out what it was. They told me it was heroin. You see, my thinking was that coke and heroin were the biggest and strongest of all drugs. I had tried 'E' with a mate, Mark, sharing it with him. This was halfway through the nineties when uppers were going out and downers were coming in. So when I was growing up there were always plenty of uppers and downers. All the ex-ravers were now into this cool drug called KIT. I was fourteen and had fallen totally in love with drugs and alcohol.

I asked this couple if I could try this drug called KIT, as they were smoking it. They gave me a toot of the last bit of heroin on the tinfoil, which they called the beetle. There I was saying to Gary and Lynn, "Don't worry, I won't tell anyone you gave this to me." I was fourteen and wanting to try all drugs. That was my ambition in life. I wasn't totally blown away with their drug. Most addicts will tell you that the first time smoking heroin, they thought they could take it or leave it, but that is a lie from the pit of hell. I just went on other drugs or alcohol, but once this drug comes into your life, it becomes your god.

While I was trying KIT now and then, I was introduced to a prescribed drug, with the street name called Tem's. Tosh and I took one in Gary and Lynn's home and that was it. I loved it. I would snort it and then smoke dope. It was the best feeling ever at that time. I was numb. I had found the answer to life.

At this age and the way I was living, I had no real interest in God. Back in Albion Street when I was about ten, I decided to go to a Catholic church called All Saints, in Coatdyke. There was some seed inside me then that made me want to go. By the time I was thirteen, all I wanted was the flesh, and nothing else. But I didn't really speak like the flesh or speak of the spirit. I thought all this stuff that pleases the flesh was the normal thing to do.

Jazza, Tosh, another one of our mates and I decided to go our own way and do our own thing. We got into buzzing gas, speed and alcohol straight away. It didn't take long until the police got into our lives. Jazza and I had broken into an empty house. It was not the first time we had done it, but the first time we had got caught, so we were taken to the police station and put in the cells until our parents came to fetch us. The house had got flooded because we were trying to pull out the water tank for the copper, to get some money, but someone had seen us and phoned the police.

That might have been my first time in the cells, but it was not my last. After that, we were making a name for ourselves, or that's what we wanted to achieve anyway, going about starting fights with other youngsters from different areas. By now I had been thrown out of St. Patrick's and had no school to go to. It just gave me more time to get myself into more trouble, drinking every day. Don't ask me why, but my aim was to be an alcoholic. Getting lifted with the police became a normal thing for us. Our goals were to get money through theft so we could buy drink and drugs.

We started fighting with different groups in areas around Coatbridge. Then Gurie began to hang around with us as well. When Gurie was younger, he had a talent for playing football. He was head and shoulders above everyone else and a lot stronger, but he got banned from playing in his early teens because he kept fighting with the guys in the other teams. He had once chased the referee round the park with a flagpole. He had the talent, but he didn't have the head for it.

Around this time, a lot of us would go to a certain nightclub in an area of Coatbridge called Redbrigg. We went for the fighting afterwards. The fights weren't planned, we just stood outside wanting to fight anyone that wasn't with us or was against us. Our gang, the Y-D, was the worst of them all. We would attack anyone there. Guys from Shawhead would join in with us too. Once we were all walking past McDonald's and one guy with us hit someone in the face with a can of lager. The man was a stranger to all of us. In a second, everyone was attacking the guy who got hit, and he was taking some kicking for nothing at all. I didn't touch the guy. All of a sudden, this other guy jumped into it, as he was the first guy's friend. So everyone in our group started giving both guys a really bad kicking. The two of them were out for the count. I thought they were dead. These two poor guys got this kicking for absolutely nothing. It was so sad.

I missed nearly all of Year Four at school. My Dad asked St Patrick's High if they would give me another chance and the school did, but not long after that they asked me to leave. You see, the other students were doing their final year exams and I wasn't interested. I was getting kicked out for taking the teacher's purse out of her bag. The school knew I wasn't going to change. At fifteen, the three other high schools wouldn't let me in. Even then I tried to get in, but the minute the head teacher read the reports from St. Patrick's, I had no chance. And the same thing happened to Tosh. So instead of school I had to go to college one and a half days a week. College in Britain is for adults who have finished high school and they go to college for further education on whatever they want to learn. I went to learn how to do joinery and my Dad was so happy for me, hoping I would enjoy it and change my life style.

Once at a children's panel, they were planning to put me into a children's home, but my Dad spoke to them during the discussions. The children's panel was for teenagers who were getting into a lot of trouble. One time they were going to put me into a children's home and my Dad said to them, "Give my son one more chance," hoping I would stop getting arrested by the police. You see, the arrests by the police were happening more when I was at my Mum's than when I was at my Dad's. My Dad managed to get them to give me another chance. Then I got lifted again, not long after the panel.

I can still remember that night getting arrested, I had been drinking and taking speed and I was shouting all kinds of not so nice things to the police. One of the police chased me and the other sat in the police car. I ran through back gardens at night, so the officer couldn't see me hiding because it was dark. I was lying down on the grass. The officer jumped over the fence next to me and didn't see me hiding. I couldn't get up and run out of the garden as there was the other officer outside the garden in the car. As the officer who was chasing me was walking back to the car, he noticed me and got a grip of me and put me in the police car to go to the police station.

FIRST ACCIDENT

On 4th May, 1996, I was drinking a bottle of wine with a group of my mates. We were all playing football (SOCCER). This day I can barely remember, but what happened was that I had seen my two sisters walking with their friend, Pauline towards the shop in Greenend. I told my mates I was going to get a cigarette. One of my mates shouted on me that he'd give me one, but I carried on, running towards my sisters.

I got to the road, and there was a large van in front of me, so I ran around it, and as I got to the other side of the road, a car hit me. My trainers flew off and I was lying unconscious on the road with a puddle of blood around my head. My sisters and Pauline were all over the place, screaming. It was like a dream, and to them I was dead. My two mates, Jazza and Tosh were on either side of me, holding my hands. A man came out of his car, carrying a football sock, and put it under the left side of my head to stop the bleeding. People were coming out of their houses to see what was happening.

The man who hit me came from Airdrie. He hadn't stopped or even skidded, but had just driven on because he was scared for his life. Two taxi drivers chased after him and got him to pull over in Sikeside. I was taken to Monklands Hospital in Airdrie, where

First Accident

they kept me breathing, and then I was transferred to the Southern General Hospital in Glasgow. I was put on a life support machine for two weeks, which kept me breathing.

For the first few days, I had wires coming in and out of me. The surgeon had to cut the left side of my skull open to do the operation. I cannot remember one single thing during this time. Once I was off the life support machine, I was taken back to Monklands Hospital. Monkland, S Apparently after I woke up, I wouldn't stop screaming for some days.

As I started to come around, I remember looking out of the window and I knew I recognized the place from somewhere. When I started speaking, all I would talk about was gangs, drugs and drink. I had had serious brain surgery. I didn't have a clue what had just happened or why. Later on, my family was allowed to take me home for the weekend in a wheelchair. I remember Gurie, Tosh and Jazza, coming to my home to see me and to watch the Scotland v. England game, and an England player called Paul Gascoigne, who played for Rangers, scoring a cracker of a goal. As he lay on the ground after scoring, some of the England players were squirting water in his mouth.

Back in the hospital, different mates would come to see me. Not long after this happened to me, some of these mates murdered a guy at Bunkums nightclub in Redbrigg. They just kicked him to death.

When I started to come around after being on the life support machine, a nurse told me about the accident. I can still remember being really bothered about nearly dying a virgin. That's a big deal to a fifteen-year-old.

My Dad's side of the family took a big concern in me, and this was my family who I thought didn't care. I'm sure my Gran and

Grandad Flynn prayed for me. They thought I was going to be crippled down one side of my body because I wasn't moving much in my right side. My Dad's family are mostly believers in the God of the Bible. I don't know too much about my Mum's side — maybe they also talk to the Lord in their quiet moments. I had the idea that you only got into heaven by your good works.

I had had an epileptic fit when coming off the life support machine. After I had this fit, people started to realize what damage the accident left me in. It's a common thing for people to take fits after serious head injuries. The accident was in May, and by July/August I was home again. One weekend when I was home with my family, about three months after the accident, my Dad and I were at my auntie's home and Dad was cutting the grass. He gave the lawnmower to me while he went upstairs to fetch something. As he looked through the window, he noticed that I was cutting the grass with the wires underneath the mower. The wires went from the lawn mower through my auntie's window to the plug to keep it going. The plug my Dad switched off was near the window he was at. I could have so easily been electrocuted with the metal blade of the lawnmower cutting through the wires on the lawn mower. He got the fright of his life, opened the window and shouted out, and then turned off the switch in the wall to stop the electricity.

My social worker had told my Dad that he should let me out rather than keep me in the house, once I got out of hospital. A week out of hospital, my Dad allowed me out to see my mates for a few hours. Even that surprised me, as I was seriously not well, badly brain-damaged, and didn't know what I was talking about. On the left side of my head there was no skull, just skin. It didn't take me long to realize that Tosh, Jazza and Gurie were different to me because

First Accident

I wasn't the same guy after the brain injury. I wouldn't stop talking, and none of it made any sense. I was like a big child. I had grown in size, probably because I had not smoked or taken drugs in that time. I was even bigger than Gurie.

Jazza, Tosh and I had tried heroin a few times, and even Gurie was into it. I think we had all got fed up with alcohol and uppers. Tosh and Jazza had turned sixteen and Gurie and I were still fifteen. It seemed like everyone I knew was into this drug KIT (heroin). Tosh and I were in a flat in Sikeside, and there was a guy there we had known all our lives. He was a man of the streets, ten years older than us, and he was smoking KIT. He offered me a line of it and I couldn't say no, even though I was just off a life-support machine. I went straight into drug addiction on cannabis every day, and it didn't take long before I was smoking heroin. Tosh couldn't believe I was smoking heroin with him and the friend who grew up very street-wise. I had had serious brain surgery and Tosh was thinking I might take a fit. Jazza and Gurie were running around feeding their own heroin addiction. There was a massive separation in our friendship, and the rejection I felt was huge. I was walking about smoking dope, sometimes heroin, and at the same time still seriously affected by the brain injury.

Most of the flats in Sikeside had been knocked down by the time I got out of the hospital. I started going out shoplifting. Even Sikeside was changing, as it was getting the flats knocked down. It didn't change me much as I was still always shoplifting. I stole aftershave from a drugstore in Coatdyke, but a woman in the shop saw me. She and a man went out in a van to get me. I had just sold it, but they took me back to the drugstore, the police came, and I got arrested. I wouldn't tell the police who I had sold it to, as the rules in the streets make you know pretty clear that telling the police anything is something you can't do, and if you do the results are violence. My Aunty and Dad went to the police station and told them about my accident, so I got out.

When I had got out of the hospital, a guy I knew gave me an air rifle. I was sitting not far from the football parks with the gun. I was speaking to God from the heart and I began to believe it was God who had saved me. I used to speak about God a lot, but I always thought about creation and Adam and Eve, and I had questions about how humans all came to be. As a kid, I had been told that we had evolved from the apes, so if that was true then not all of the Bible was true. I always believed in the resurrection of Christ, and to me the devil was red and had horns coming out of the sides of his head.

Little did I know that Satan was an angel and that when he was thrown out of heaven, a third of the angels went with him. At one point before he became Satan, he had been the apple of God's eye. Pride kicked in and Lucifer, who became the devil, thought he was equal to God. The word of God to me was pretty frightening then. I was worried, in case I didn't believe what I read. I can remember the basics the Catholic church had taught me, but I thought God was up in the air and Satan was below me. I actually got closer to God after the accident. I don't know the exact reason for that, but I do believe when I was on the life support machine a lot of people were praying for me, and God had heard those prayers and answered them. Surgeons are great at what they do and God uses them, but I do believe it is God who gets the final say.

All the ravers had stopped by this time and no one seemed to care about the music. Everyone used to love taking "E," speed or L.S.D., but now everyone just cared for themselves. I believe all the gangsters had planned this long before it happened. It was hard for the ex-ravers to get valium or temazepam; all they could get was the drug everyone said they would never take — heroin.

I was sixteen and I asked Sean and my Aunty Jean if I could come and live with them until I got into rehabilitation for people with head injuries in Bonkle. You see, I was still really not well after the accident, and it was going to take years to get better. The brain takes a long time to heal. I used to go out and kick a ball about outside their home, and one night two young women came over to me and paid attention to me. Sean and Aunty Jean had moved from Kilsyth to Croy, a village known for being a Catholic village, just as Harthill where my Dad and Patricia stayed was Protestant. One of the young women wanted to meet me again, so I told her to call at my house the next evening. So the next evening they came over. One of them liked me and she had made an effort to look good.

Croy was a place where everyone knew each other, and I was like the new kid on the block. As I got talking to them, more young women appeared and some of them took an interest in me. I actually had a choice. I picked one of them and she came across as she liked me, so I kissed her at the back of the house, then she asked me to go for a walk with her, so I did. She took me near a golf course and we had sex. I had lost my virginity. That was me, the happiest guy about, no longer the virgin. It was the best few minutes of my life. Little did I know that it was the start of me becoming a sex addict. Yes, a sex addict. Before the accident, I was pretty shy with women, but after the accident I wanted sex. The young woman was called Lisa and she did not realize that I was not well.

Not long after that, I got the invitation to start at Bonkle Rehabilitation Centre, which helps people after brain injuries. It was a really nice place, like a small hotel. I ended up spending most of my time in the smokers' room. The staff took classes that helped the brain heal, but my thinking was that time would heal me. I was a terrible listener, even at school. I always had a lot of energy in me and just wanted to do my own thing. I was a bit hyper.

I remember this guy came in who had been brought up in an area of Glasgow called Royston, a Catholic part. He told me that he moved about a lot, going to different countries, and at one point had lived in Sweden. He was a pretty cool sort of a guy and this was his second time in this rehab place. I remember him telling me that he had looked up the history of the Bible and could prove that it wasn't true. He told me that he believed in evolution and I asked him what religion that was. He didn't believe there was a God. This guy had a very painful leg and he liked his cannabis to ease the pain, so we sometimes went together to get a smoke. I liked this guy. He was one of the first guys I had met who had been in trouble but had changed, and I liked the way he spoke about peace. It was 1997 and this guy was telling me that Jesus was true, but he was just a man claiming to be the Son of God.

While I was in Bonkle, my Dad's side of the family made an effort to come and visit me. At the weekends, I would go to Croy and visit Sean and Aunty Jean, but I also wanted to see that young woman and have a drink with her and her mates. Then there was only one thing on my mind, and that was sex. I was getting a lot of attention. This girl named Lisa liked me, but I was not that bothered about her. I started kissing one of her mates behind her back. One weekend we had a drink in one of her mates' homes, and this new girl showed an interest in me, so I finished with Lisa and went with her mate. Lisa was crying and was really let down by me. The next

First Accident

day, the same girl came to Sean's house to see me, but when we went out for a walk, she realized I was not well from the accident as I wasn't making any sense. To me, it was just the way I was, wanting girls for sex. Changing myself for the better was something that was not on my mind. I would talk about the crime I was doing and boasting about the gang fights. I was actually a decent young man, but I wanted to be like all the ones who were doing all the things that were against the law.

Whether God was above me, below me, inside me — I don't know. All I know is that He was with me, looking after me. You see, He had a plan and a purpose for my life. I had just turned seventeen when I left the center at Bonkle, even though they said they should have given me longer than six months. I met a girl through Sean's son and she was from Kilsyth, near Croy. I was with her and was drinking when a gang of young guys from that area started on me. I said to one of them that if he had a problem, let's sort it out, and a fight broke out, me versus them. They got me down and started laying the kicks into me.

Remember, I had a hole in the side of my head from when it was opened up during the brain surgery, but these guys didn't know that. Suddenly, they all turned and ran as the police had arrived. They must have been passing by in a car, or else the good Lord brought them over to save my life. I was going off my head, so I got lifted and was put in a cell. My cousin from Sikeside was now living in Kilsyth with his partner and son, so he came down to speak to the police and I got out.

Not long after that, I decided to go back to Coatbridge and stay with my Dad. It wasn't long before heroin came back into my life. Jazza and I halved in for a £10 bag of heroin. Tosh was with us.

There was no tin foil in Jazza's Mum's house, so Tosh and I shared my half, while Jazza injected his £5 half. I didn't know what exactly to feel, as I had never injected any drug before. I wasn't totally blown away with it, but I liked the warm feeling it gave me. There was no need for me to smoke now that I could inject. No going back now.

There was a cafe in Bellshill that could help me find full-time work. It was for people who had suffered head injuries, and it provided training and then fixed up a job for them. My social worker, Steve, took part in this scheme, but he told me I was probably the worst client he had had because of the number of charges I had. But now that I was injecting heroin, I could only learn how to work at the cafe rather than move on to a proper job.

One day at the café, I was sitting after lunch along with a guy from Motherwell, who was doing his probation there. He began telling me this story about how he had fought two guys in Whifflet. As he went on, I realized the two guys he was describing were me and Jazza. This is what happened: We were all fighting a gang one night, and Jazza and Gurie got one guy. Jazza broke a bottle and slashed one guy. The two of them got lifted for it, and at fifteen, instead of going to children's panels, they had to go to court. But the story this guy was telling was not long after the slashing. Jazza and I were down in Greenend in a house when three people from our area who we knew well went into the kitchen and had a hit of heroin. That was the first time I had seen anyone hit up heroin, and Jazza and I were fifteen at the time. The two of us left the house and went to Whifflet in Coatbridge. As we were walking past one guy and two girls, the guy started saying stuff to us, so Jazza and I started squaring up to him. Nothing happened.

As we walked on, we saw a group of guys we knew and we told them about him, and then we all went back and found the guy standing in a bus stop — the same man from Motherwell. Then this fight broke out, but the guy me and Jazza were nearly fighting with was in the bus stop and had a broken bottle in his hand and he slashed it down the side of the guy's face. It was a really bad slashing down his face. The man from Motherwell fell on Jazza and started to slash Jazza, splitting his lip in two. I separated the two and stopped a taxi, put the two in the taxi, and off we went to Monklands Hospital. They left a trail of blood in reception and the nurses took them away to get stitches. The police came in, and as I was speaking to them, the guy who had done the slashing walked into the hospital. I identified him to the police. Why am I telling this story about Jazza slashing one guy and not long after getting slashed himself? A man reaps what he sows. (Galatians ch.6 v.7)

So this guy from Motherwell, who was now talking, was the one who had done the slashing. As soon as I told him that I was one of the guys he was speaking of, the first thing he said was that he was really sorry and he was not really like that. It was just that when he got drunk, he changed from the nice guy I was talking to into someone very different.

My family all found out that I was injecting heroin. When you are an addict, you don't realize what you put your family through. For parents to find out that their son or daughter has become a heroin addict is heart-breaking for them. There are fathers, mothers, brothers and sisters who have lost their loved ones through these evil addictions. It is so easy to pick this stuff up, but getting out of it is so hard. I am so grateful that my family always stuck by me and always continued to keep me in their prayers. God listens.

Before my family found out I was using heroin, I went to the Southern General Hospital to have a metal plate put in the side of my head. I was expecting that after the operation I would wake up and all would be good. But I wasn't expecting the pain. It is hard to describe just how painful it was. I certainly hadn't been expecting that.

While in the hospital, I met a man from Govan in Glasgow. He was homeless with nowhere to go, so he sat in the smoking area of the hospital. After my operation, I met him and found out that he took heroin, so I gave him a few packets of cigarettes, which he sold, to get a bag of heroin. We went into the toilets and had a hit. Honestly, I fell in love even more with this drug. I loved the way it made me feel and felt a protection and comfort from it. Apart from my mate Mark, who didn't get into it, all my other mates became junkies. We thought of no one but ourselves. I remember smashing up a junkie's home earlier, not knowing that one day I would be one myself.

My family didn't know where to turn, so they went to a Narcotics Anonymous meeting in Glasgow. There they were told not to give me a roof over my head or feed me, or I wouldn't want to get my life sorted out. They were told to let me hit rock bottom and then I would want to change. There is a lot of truth in that. My family was also told to pray to their God to look after me, but they were not to make life easy for me. Addicts walk all over people who are a soft touch. It is the nature of addiction.

I also caught Hepatitis C at seventeen, through sharing dirty needles. By eighteen years of age, my life was a total mess. Full of paranoia, eight stone in weight, 112 pounds, just skin and bones, it felt as though the world was against me. I had not properly recovered from the accident at fifteen. Do you know the crazy thing about being paranoid? I didn't even know it was me being paranoid, the lies in my head seemed so true.

One day Paddy, another guy, and I were in a park. We had valleys (valium) and Paddy was on the drink. My mate and I were going to inject the valleys in a two ml. syringe. My mate got hot water from his Mum and Dad's, so we found a wee quiet part of the park. He injected his first. It was a cold day and I could hardly see a vein, so I decided to let him inject me in my groin like he had just done to himself. So I took my trousers down and he stuck the needle into my groin, pulled it back, and all I could see was this pink blood flying into the needle. He then started to push the drug into my artery. I was screaming with pain, but he just carried on doing it. He then said it was because I he hadn't broken up the valleys. He pulled back the syringe and the pink blood went flying back into the syringe and then he pushed the blood back into my artery. It was so painful, I can't describe it. The second time was just as painful as the first.

I couldn't walk right, but I managed to get home to my two sisters, who were drinking with their friend, Pauline. I just went straight to bed, knocked out with the pain. My sisters were surprised I didn't go into the living room and sit with them, because that was what I always did, but this time I was in serious pain. When I woke, I was so paralyzed with pain I couldn't walk, so my sisters called an ambulance to take me to hospital. I told the doctor what had happened, and he gave me a tub of painkillers and sent me home.

It didn't take long before this big bubble started to grow out from my groin, and I could see the poison in it. The bubble grew and so did the pain. In hospital again, they wanted to put a long needle down my leg to get the poison out, but I refused. After four weeks of this pain, I woke one morning to find the pain had stopped, but there was a really strong smell as if something had died in the room and had been there a while. I pulled down my covers and saw that my belly and all down my leg were covered in green and yellow poison. A lot of the poison wasn't all inside my body, but a lot came out after the bubble burst in my sleep, and I could see the poison all over my belly and leg.

My Aunty Jessy, my Mum's oldest sister, drove me to hospital and I was operated on. Afterwards, the doctor told me the poison had travelled all the way down to my toe and the operation should have been done before the bubble burst. She added that if it hadn't burst, they would have had to cut my leg off, or I could have died with the poison.

The man who had injected me in my artery was in a house in Greenend with me, and I was drinking. He was diabetic and had no insulin. I didn't know much about his body needing sugar. There were a few of us there and one of us turned to my mate and saw he was sitting on his chair dead. I wasn't angry with him for injecting the drug into my artery, and I wasn't pleased to see him dead, even though I nearly died with what he had done to me. He knew what he was doing to me when he injected the drug and the blood into my artery. He could hear me screaming, plus the blood in my artery was pink, not red. We phoned an ambulance, but when the paramedics came in to see what they could do, we could tell that they knew he was dead by just looking at his skin, which was bright yellow, not pale white.

I was eighteen and had heard about Methadone some time before, but the important thing I knew was that it was free. To me, it was nothing to do with stopping heroin. In 1998/99, I got put on 50ml., which was a lot then. After that, I could get my Methadone, go

First Accident

home to my Dad's and smoke dope. I knew if I was getting a smoke of dope, I wouldn't go out to get heroin, because it filled my head with fear. And that was me doing good! My Dad would go to his woman's and I would sit in with my Methadone and get a smoke.

My first time getting thrown out of home was at that same time. It was only for about four weeks, but even that was dreadful. Tosh and another man and I would sleep in a two-man tent. Scotland can be pretty wet and cold. I was very mixed up with life, very insecure, and believed a lot of lies very easily. I always felt out of place, but I know now why, and that's because God didn't make me for that sort of lifestyle. None of us are made that way. No one was made to live a dark life. God made us to be His. God wants to free us from the lies of the devil that say, "How can God love you? Look what you have done and remember the way you were thinking."

I can remember one day sitting in my sister's bedroom, an addict, just skin and bones and my life a mess. I got on my knees and started speaking to the Lord from the heart. God doesn't say that when we're off drugs He'll listen. God heard my voice. Nothing supernatural happened to me, but God was with me.

PSALM 130 v. 1–4 says, "Out of the depths I cry to you, O Lord; O Lord, hear my voice. Let your ears be attentive to my cry for mercy. If you, O Lord, kept a record of sins, O Lord, who could stand? But with you there is forgiveness; therefore you are feared."

God tells us in His word to become like little children. I was thinking of that. When children hurt themselves, the first thing they do is put out their hands so their parents can reach out to cuddle them and reassure them. It is like that for Christians. We are told in the Bible that we all have storms and enemies, but we can reach out to God; He is our comforter, our protector and our peace.

I spent many years going about, thinking that I could do so much better than the way I was living. With most addictions, you need help to find out why you do it. You can't just leave heroin, it's not that easy. A good friend said that we were not bad people trying to be good, but sick people trying to get well. I could never give my racing mind a rest. It used to go a million miles an hour and my mind was full of broken bottles. I wanted to do good and be a guy who could walk about and not get looked at as a junkie. I hated that. In my heart, I was always seeking the Lord. I wanted Him to be true, but I had so many questions about things in the Bible, Adam and Eve, Noah and the flood. It confused me. Now I don't understand one hundred percent, but I believe it to be true.

FIRST EXPERIENCE OF THE CHRISTIAN LIFE

My Dad had thrown me out and I had nowhere to go. My Aunt Jean heard about this and spoke to her man, Sean, about it. Sean had given his life to the Lord and had become a born again Christian by this time, so Sean and Aunty Jean agreed that I could go and live with them in Croy. The agreement was that if I used heroin again, I would have to leave. At that time I was on 50 ml. Methadone. My thinking was that it was okay to still take drugs and drink, as long as I got my Methadone. If I didn't inject heroin, then everything would be okay.

Sean had been attending a Christian church. This church had a vision called G12, which I knew nothing about. All I knew about churches was that they wanted your money and they messed with your head. I remember watching Christian preachers on TV praying over people and seeing them fall to the ground. Some said it was real, some said it was actors trying to get money out of you. I felt a fear inside when Sean took me to this church. It was definitely not what I was used to in the Catholic church where I had been brought up. It seemed extreme. I saw women walking up and down praying, and a young man kneeling down with his arm going up and down as if he was banging the seat of a chair, but to me it didn't look right.

I met some ex-addicts there. I had never met any ex-heroin addicts who had got clean and found God. These guys didn't smoke or drink, or chase after women, which seemed strange to me. They said they were waiting on God to give them a partner. All this was very new to me. One of the ex-addicts I met had got released from jail, gone to this church and been touched by the Holy Spirit. He was jumping about with joy. Another guy from Easterhouse in Glasgow's east end, not far from Coatbridge, found God after heroin addiction. He was a young man who wanted to serve the Lord. I looked up to these guys and wanted what they had. I went to the church, not every week, but I didn't really listen to what the preacher was saying.

At the Tuesday meetings, the church split into small groups, and during one meeting my group leader explained how he had been caught importing drugs, though he said he had never taken heroin himself, and how he had later become a Christian. Later on in life, I found out that some of his testimony was exaggerated and I found it hard to take him seriously. I moved into Sean's small group later on. His group met in Kilsyth and I was surprised that this leader let addicts into his home and didn't judge us. I had met a woman from Kilsyth and she attended one of these meetings with us. We were praying and some people were speaking this language I couldn't understand. They called it praying in tongues. This girl and I couldn't stop laughing.

The man leading the meeting said that he believed taking Methadone to be wrong. I was off heroin for a few months, but I was taking Temazepam and Valium nearly every day. I was always looking over my shoulder because I knew trouble was going to happen through my own addictions. The idea of surrendering my life to the Lord was a no chance. That was too hard to do. I wanted to believe that sleeping around was okay, and that being on Methadone along with taking other drugs was okay. It suited me fine. After all, everyone else was doing it.

One weekend in Kilsyth, I met up with a woman I had already been with. I was drinking and taking drugs. This younger guy started trouble. He was shouting about the women I was with, saying that the woman was his mate's girlfriend. And because he was still shouting and causing trouble by shouting at me, we started arguing and I began to swing this guy about, when a car drove up with these guys in it. I started running, chased by the guy I had been fighting and another guy. I ended up behind a bank, but I was worn out. I can't remember much, but I got a kicking. I shouted down at them so they ran back up to me. I ran on to the middle of the road and got one of them down, but the other one pushed me from behind and I fell. They were at either side of me, laying kicks into me as I was trying to protect my head and face. They did not know that I had a plate in the left hand side of my skull. They broke my elbow, but suddenly they stopped and ran off as the police happened to be driving past. This was not far from the place I got a kicking when I was seventeen. The police took me back to Sean and Jean's, and later I went to Monklands Hospital and got a stookie (plaster cast) on my arm for two weeks. I believe it was God who brought the police to the kicking I was getting. One bad kick to my head could easily have killed me. Not long after that I went to Coatbridge to meet up with Jazza and do all I knew, get heroin and get a hit. By this time I was nearly twenty-one and my life was still in a total mess.

Redemption through the blood

Back in Croy, Sean and I had a big argument and Sean asked me to leave. I went to this woman's home, the girl I had been going with. After being in Croy for eight or nine months and then in Kilsyth for a fortnight, I decided to go back to my Dad's in Coatbridge, and was happy to be back there. My time in Croy and Kilsyth had not been great and I always felt I didn't belong there. A lot of people didn't like me because I was looked on as a junkie. They didn't even try to get to know me. I left thinking about that guy who had been touched by the Holy Spirit in the church in Cumbernauld. I wanted that, because in my heart I always wanted to believe the whole Bible and not just some bits. I knew I needed God to show me that He was real. Giving up the label of being a Catholic and becoming a Christian was something I couldn't do then.

SUICIDE

It wasn't long before I was back in Coatbridge, living the same sort of life. I was in my mate Joe's house in Greenend, thinking how much I was sick of life and that I didn't want this life anymore. I had been drinking and I wanted to end it all. As I was walking home, I was thinking about salvation. When I got home, my Dad and I were shouting at each other, so I went to my big sister's room to find her shaver, got the blade out of it and slit my wrist really deeply. The blood squirted out fast and soon made a big puddle in the room. I started screaming and my youngest brother, Steven (Dad and Patricia's son) came into the room, followed by my Dad, who quickly put towels round my wrist to stop the blood flow. An ambulance came and took me to Monklands Hospital, checked the flow and took me to theatre to operate on my wrist. Following the operation, I needed twenty-five staples and I had a stookie on my wrist. Again, my Dad had saved me from bleeding to death. The doctors said to my Dad if he didn't help stop the bleeding, I would have bled to death as I would have lost too much blood.

It was a nice day, so I decided to walk to my Aunt Jessie's. As I walked, there was a woman walking in front of me. She stopped, turned around, and said she didn't like people walking behind her.

We got talking. She had a plastic bottle with some wine in it, called Buckfast. Coatbridge had a reputation for people drinking a lot of this wine and then getting in a lot of trouble. She told me her name was Dangerous Diane. That didn't bother me. Everyone I knew was dangerous anyway. But I did want a drink of her Buckfast. We spent the whole day together, and in the evening she went back to her family in Wishaw, about thirty minutes away by car.

I happened to know some of her family from Coatbridge and they knew me. I had used drugs with one of her cousins a few times. Dangerous was a Catholic, but most of the guys she ran about with in Wishaw were Protestants, and they didn't really like the Catholics. Dangerous had two lovely kids who were harmless, but she had a reputation for going with guys who hit her. I got the impression she was called Dangerous because of her mouth more than anything else. It's a small world. Her mum and my Mum had been in the same class at school. I met a lot of crazy women, but Dangerous Diane floats to the top. Most of her mates didn't like me. She was the type of woman who could start a fight in an empty room. A lot of trouble came my way through her. She knew I wouldn't lift my hand to her, so she would attack me. Violence also came my way through her mouth.

I was in Coatbridge with a mate and went into my Dad's, who told me I had been awarded £30,000 compensation for my accident when I got run over. If I hadn't had a criminal record and been on Methadone, I would have received more like £250,000, so the report said that the accident hadn't changed me much. But I didn't care. I was happy with the £30,000. Not long after that, I was with Dangerous Diane at my Mum's when the police came looking for me, just wanting to talk to me. So Diane and I went to the station and Diane sat in reception while I went into an interview room. They had heard that I had thirty grand coming in. The guy I was with must have told people and it had got back to the police. You see, the police knew I had money coming in, so it was clear to them that a lot of drugs were going to be getting bought and took by the drug addicts in Coatbridge. The police were telling me that they knew about the money and they would be watching me.

Not long after that, the money came in, so Diane and I did what we knew best — got plenty of alcohol. Of course she was holding the money, and I'm sure she was very generous to her mates. One night the two of us had a fall-out and she fetched her uncle over. Not that I had done anything wrong, but she just started trouble. So her uncle came in and was sitting in kitchen where we were. He asked me to go outside and he got me from the back, pulled me down to the grass and started laying the boot in. He left. I didn't care. I got up and got a taxi back to my Dad's. As I was driving away, Diane was standing at the window. I think she knew I wasn't coming back. The money she had was just a small amount. The rest of my money was in my bank account.

Because I was in Wishaw, I missed court. I'm not sure what the charge was for. I don't think it was for anything really serious, no doubt something like theft out of a shop, so I had warrants out for me, plus the police knew about the money I had. I decided to disappear from Coatbridge, so my Dad came up with an idea. We ended up in a small village called Cardross, near Helensburgh, a town I knew a little. I had been cut off from my Methadone by this time and my main addiction was alcohol. My Dad was hoping that my life would change for the better now. Changing towns and having money just wasn't enough. I didn't really care about the money I had, and I was into drinking at that time. I would give up drugs, start drinking day and night, then get bored with that and start using drugs again. It was a vicious circle. I would sit in a pub in Cardross from morning till night, depressed and drinking. I always hoped the next drink would give me back my confidence, but it never did.

I was in a pub in Helensburgh and this guy was selling CDs. I knew straightaway this guy was into the same drugs as I was into. We got talking. He had started off with heroin, but it wasn't giving him the same hit, so he got into hitting up coke. A few weeks later, we went to an area of Glasgow called Townhead. I gave him the money for heroin and coke. We got to some high flats and I gave him a half gram of the coke while I had the other half. He was injecting into his groin, but I still had plenty of veins left in my arm. While I was trying to get a vein in my arm, this guy had already injected his and was staggering all over the place with his trousers down, blood running down his leg, and a 2 ml. needle hanging from his groin. This was the first time I started freaking out after injecting coke, and I was thinking all the young ones from that area were going to walk in and give us a kicking. I couldn't wait to get to a toilet somewhere to do the heroin, because I knew it would bring me down from the coke. You walk about on that stuff and you can feel everyone's eyes on you.

Another time, we were in Dumbarton walking past a shop and there was an addict standing at the door. He asked if we had some spare money, so I opened my wallet to give him some. There was £300 in my wallet and this guy saw the money and followed us. We got to this dealer's home and the two of us walked in. I had never been here before and I didn't know the other guys in the house. I told the dealer what I wanted and pulled out my wallet to pay for the drugs. The guy I had given a few pounds to, when he had been standing outside the shop, now ran up behind me and grabbed the wallet. I wouldn't let go of it until I saw from the corner of my eye another guy pull out a knife, so I let the wallet go. The two guys split the money and gave me back £40 for four bags of heroin. Very nice of them.

I met a woman there called Laura. She didn't take drugs, but drank nearly every day. The two of us had one thing in common. We thought everyone who passed us was talking about us. Laura was on tablets for this. I didn't realize what was wrong with me, but thought everyone was talking about me too. I was in Cardross for just three months and still thought everyone was bad-mouthing me because I was always drunk. The landlord of the bed and breakfast I was staying in asked me to leave. They probably realized I was on heroin, as well as regularly being drunk. No matter where I was or who I was with, I always felt out of place. That was because God hadn't created me to be that way.

I left with Laura to go back to Coatbridge again. I had bought a fisherman's knife off a guy in Helensburgh, as I liked the look of it. Laura and I were walking to Greenend, and all we saw were guys I knew from there, running from the police. I remembered there was a warrant out for me, and there I was, carrying a knife. So I put my hand in the inside pocket of my jacket, grabbed the knife, and as I threw it away the police saw what I was doing. They grabbed me, picked up the knife, and took me to the police station. It was a Friday too. Now getting lifted with the police and getting caught with a knife, plus having a warrant out for you is definitely court on Monday. On Monday, I went to the Sheriff's Court and got out on bail. Many people in Coatbridge, mostly addicts, knew I had this money. If I'm honest, I was very insecure and vulnerable and my head was a total mess. And having that sort of money, living that life and being insecure and vulnerable, left me open to getting money taken from me.

Around this time, I lost the love for drugs, but I couldn't stop. I was an addict, obsessed with these addictions, and I couldn't just turn this addiction off and go live a decent life. This stuff had left me sick.

I met up with a guy from Coatbridge I had known most of my life. He liked coke, but I was more into heroin. One day we were in a house doing coke. He didn't inject but I did, so I went upstairs, had a hit of the coke, came downstairs, went into the living room and started running up and down the living room. Then I fell on the floor and took a fit. This guy got the fright of his life.

The more I took coke, the more I thought everyone's eyes were on me. It was like my confidence was shattered. I was full of fear. I had to get downers just to bring me down from major paranoia. Everywhere I went, I could feel people looking at me, as if they could tell how I was feeling. I was one of those guys who couldn't hide how I was feeling. I didn't really care about the money. I just wanted away from this sick life. The only people who really cared for me were my family, and all I did was let them down and leave them worried about me. Life on the streets is a very selfish thing. Addicts care for one thing above all else, and that is to get their next hit, even if that means stealing from your own family to feed your habit.

I always thought about God when I was in a dark place. I would hope that one day I could believe all the Bible, because I struggled to believe some parts of it. You see, I had a wee idea of the Bible because Catholic schools teach you about the Lord God. And also I would think about the church I had been to. The people I met there were intelligent and they believed the Bible to be true.

I had this money, and back in Coatbridge I was in a house using drugs, and one guy, Richard, came up to me. I had known Richard all of my life, as he was a Sikeside man. I used to buy my drugs off him. This time he was selling coke and he knew I had money.

Once I was in a car with him and three other guys from Coatbridge. Richard had bags of coke. He stopped the car, and Richard got out to sell some coke to people in a second car. A guy from our car went over to the other car too, and without Richard noticing, picked up his bags of coke and came back to our car. Then Richard saw his coke had gone and started demanding his coke back. There was an argument about the coke going missing. Richard got back in the car and drove back to Sikeside. He got out of the car, walked to the back door, opened it, pulled out a knife and tried to slash the guy's face. He got him, but not as much as he wanted to. The other guy got out and also pulled out a knife and started chasing him, but he got away. So guess what happened? I had plenty of money. Richard had just been ripped off with coke. I became his best friend because I had the money to help him get back on his feet. It didn't take long before I was skint (no money) and had no more mates. Life of an addict — I had had £30,000 and within six months I had not a penny.

After the money was spent, I became very lonely. My Dad was raging at the guys who had spent a lot of it, and he considered taking things into his own hands, but in fact he was just happy that I was still alive after using the amount of drugs I had taken. My two arms were black and blue with injecting. I could handle the physical side of the withdrawals, but the mental side was a different matter. For days, I couldn't sleep. I watched a movie called "Saving Private Ryan," where one of the soldiers said that if God is for, us then who can be against us? I didn't understand exactly what that meant, but it always stuck in my head. My heart was saying to God, "Lord, please come and help me, please be real to me. I hate this life." You see, I always knew I could do much better. I always wanted to be a man who helped people. All this "I want to be known as a bad boy" had left me. Now I wanted to be the real me, a decent man.

The woman I had met in Helensburgh moved to her sister's in London, so on my twenty-third birthday, I decided to go to London for a few days. I didn't have much money, but enough to get there. The first thing I wanted was heroin, so I had to find someone who could get some for me. I saw a guy who looked as if he was homeless. He was drinking a can of Tennants Super and I thought he might be from Glasgow and he was. He said he could get me some heroin and he made a phone call, got me two bags and I gave him one of them. He had got them from two guys who I thought were Jamaican. I spent a few days there and missed my bus back home, so I decided to go and steal more alcohol, but this time I got caught.

It was a Friday and I was feeling withdrawals coming from drugs and alcohol. There was a warrant out for me in Scotland for missing court. Police from Coatbridge came down by plane to take me back to Coatbridge Police Station. They laughed about the London police calling me "Mr. Flynn." "You won't be called that in here," they said, and threw me in a freezing cold cell and gave me a blanket.

When I got to court the next day, my Dad was there, helping as always. He spoke to the Procurator Fiscal and I got another chance, for they had been planning to put me in prison. I lived in a lot of areas in the west of Scotland, and while there I didn't use as much heroin, so I was in less trouble with the police. When I returned to Coatbridge I would get into more crime, mostly through theft.

PRISON LIFE

January 2004. I was with a mate, Big Jim. I had just got myself a bag of heroin and I was coming down the stairs of a flat, when I spotted two police officers at the bottom of the stairs. I had this bag of heroin in my hand and I had a feeling that these officers were waiting on me because I had another warrant out for me. The police told me to stand against the wall, so they could do a warrant check. As I leaned back on the wall, I dropped the bag, and while they were doing the warrant check, I knelt down, picked up the bag, and managed to get it in my mouth without them noticing.

I knew I had a warrant out, so it was court again the next day and there was my Dad, waiting as always. I got remanded to Barlinnie Prison. Prison honestly didn't frighten me. I was used to that life and I would have known people there. I was still a mess coming off all those drugs I had taken with that £30,000. I was in the same cell as a guy I knew from my area. He didn't take drugs, but was known for selling lots of it. I was in prison for sixteen days. The one thing I didn't like about prison was that there were no clean needles, and I missed the women.

The minute I got out, I was back to the same life because that was all I knew. Two or three weeks later, I stole some alcohol from a supermarket, but as I was walking out I saw a woman who knew me because I knew her boyfriend. She knew what I was doing and I could see she noticed I had something up my jacket, so I took it out of my jacket, put it down and then walked out. Now when a security guard knows there is a thief going about, they contact each other in the different shops. I wasn't aware of this, so as I went into another shop to steal clothes, I noticed I was being watched. So I walked to another shop nearby and stole a vacuum cleaner. No one had noticed in the shop, but as I walked away with it, I spotted a police camera on me. I saw the camera moving everywhere I walked. I just carried on walking, and as I was passing the shop where I had tried to steal clothes, a woman came out of the shop and grabbed me. Before I could do anything, two police officers were running to get me.

So it was prison again, something I was going to have to get used to. I needed help to get well. I got three weeks remand in Barlinnie again, and then it was back to court. I probably would have got sentenced. I hated being locked in because I was so used to going about doing my own thing.

Round about this time, I decided I was sick and tired of this life of drugs and drink and everything it brought into my life. I got onto my knees and spoke to God about how much I wanted to change and wanted Him to be real to me. My Mum came up to visit, but I didn't know what to expect. She had something to tell me. She spoke to me about Sean and about a guy he knew who could get me into a Christian re-habilitation center called The Haven. It used to be in a program called Teen Challenge, and was still associated with that organization and run in a similar way. My Mum told me there were no women there, just men, and that we couldn't smoke. That was a bit of a surprise. (I had tried secular re-habilitation, but was thrown out after ten days.) My Mum told me that Dad had gone to Harthill to live and had given the house to my sister, so the only person to take me in was my Mum, until I got a place at The Haven. She warned me that if I took drugs or alcohol while living with her, she would throw me out and then I wouldn't be able to go to The Haven. The only problem with all this was that I had money in my account, and it was a lot to ask of me, to be out of prison with money and not to start using again.

I spent three weeks in prison sharing a cell with the same guy. He had his jail number tattooed on his chest and would brag about the crimes he had committed in Glasgow to feed his habit. By this time, all that sort of lifestyle and all that bad boy talk had left me. I hated the whole lifestyle of addiction. It had lost its attraction to me. I hated being looked at as a junkie. I always made an effort to look clean and half decent, but drugs were my god and I couldn't just turn this habit off.

When I got out of prison, the first thing I did was go and score heroin, even though I knew I had to stay clean and sober. My Mum told me she didn't want me in her home while I was using. I wanted to go to The Haven, but I also wanted to use. When I got to my Mum's that night, she wouldn't let me in, as she could tell I was on drugs, so I ended up in the high flats in Coatbridge, using and drinking. The man who lived in the flat was a Sikeside man who had spent most of his life in and out of prison, and I ran about with his nephew, who lived near my Mum's home. The man asked me to walk his nephew home and then I could go back to spend the night at his flat.

I was full of whisky and heroin, and my plan was to walk his nephew home, and then as I walked past my Mum's, I was going to put a brick through my Mum's window. That was the voice of Satan, telling me to do that as it was her fault I had ended up like this. You see, Satan didn't want me to go to The Haven and get to know Jesus. I got to the bottom of the flat and the first road we got to, I ran out and got hit by a van. God put the van in my way because I was going down to put a brick through my Mum's window. The van had hit me on one side of my body. I was lying in the road, and when the ambulance came, I refused to get in as I had alcohol left in the house I had just left.

It was late at night, and my cousin and her boyfriend were driving by. My cousin got out and told me to get into the ambulance. My Mum and Aunt Jessie had already arrived at the hospital. The nurses were trying to assess me and check what damage was done to the side of my body where the van had hit me, but I managed to get up and out of the hospital, and my Aunt Jessie drove me back to my Mum's. The next day when I woke, I really needed a drink, but I couldn't walk. My Mum asked a man she knew in the same flats if he would take me back to Monklands Hospital, and there I had to apologize for my behavior the previous night. I had injured the right side of my body but it wasn't really so bad. I knew it was God who had brought that van to stop me smashing my Mum's window. You see, God had plans for my life. If I had broken the window, then I would have gone straight to prison, plus it would have broken my Mum's heart. I knew then that God had a hedge of protection around me and had plans for my life. I spent three weeks at my Mum's, and during that time I attended some Alcoholics Anonymous meetings, enjoyed them and found hope there. I understood that I didn't have to live that way anymore. These people kept it real.

The Haven is at Kilmacolm, an amazing place, very open and green, with plenty of farmland. I went for my interview there and it seemed to be a great place to get my life together. It wasn't what I was used to, which was high tenement flats and plenty of crime everywhere. I thought that if I was at The Haven, people in Coatbridge wouldn't know where I was. I was waiting on The Haven to take me. I was wanting to leave my past in the past and start a new way of life.

I was in my brother's room one night when I woke up, unable to breathe. It felt as if something was stuck in my throat and I thought I was going to die. My Mum heard me choking and she held me and tried to help me cough it up. In the end, I swallowed it and felt it go down my throat and was able to go back to sleep. The next day, one of the guys from AA explained that it was a panic attack. I continued getting these attacks for quite a few years after that. It always happened while I was sleeping, and I would wake up with something stopping me breathing.

9TH APRIL, 2004: THE HAVEN

One of the workers in The Haven drove me to the program. I got there early in the morning and the first resident I met was a man who liked to get up early to spend time with God. He became a good friend. The program is designed to last between eleven and eighteen months. The one thing I knew about it was that it was going to be totally different from my past life.

The main problem for me was that I was not a good listener, but rather, I was a good talker. What I should have done was ditch my past and learn a new way of living. Did I do less talking and learn to listen? No!

I loved the peace of this part of Scotland, so it was 'Goodbye, Coatbridge.' I had to get to know the residents. Some I liked more than others. Also there were some who didn't have any interest in God, whereas others were wanting to follow the Lord's ways. I remember at the start that one of the teachers explained that Jesus and the Bible were a few hundred years before Islam ever came about. I would look at the staff members and wish I was where they were. I couldn't wait until I'd finished, got out and regained my freedom to go places without permission. But my life before The

Haven wasn't exactly living in freedom. Still, I was counting the days and the months.

I tried to find out how much God loved me and then work out how to love God back. I was full of lust and religion, and trying to find a loving God. I remember a man visited us from a church in Glasgow, and he told us that Catholics needed to be born again. I was puzzled about how I could love a God who doesn't give other believers the Holy Spirit. If that was true, I was going to struggle to love this God, because my family knew Jesus and prayed to the same God. Also, some of the others strongly believed you could lose your salvation. I got a bit mixed up. Some residents took this teaching with a pinch of salt, but I took it very seriously. You see, me giving up being a Catholic was something I could never see myself doing, as that was one big label I put on myself. I saw myself as better than Protestants. I knew I had to get rid of that way of thinking if I wanted to change.

Another of my big questions was the Big Bang theory. I had always believed we came from apes, as I had been taught that as a child. At The Haven, we would all go into the church we had there and we would sing Christian songs to the Lord. I wasn't all that comfortable putting my hands up to the Lord as we sang, because that was all very new to me. I was a bit nervous about reading the Bible, as I wasn't sure what I was going to get out of it. I hadn't been there long when one chapter caught my attention — Psalm 22, written by King David. I asked one of the staff, David Black, what it meant, and he explained that it was about the coming of Jesus, but King David had written about it a thousand years before it happened. *My God, my God, why have you forsaken me? Why are you so far from saving me, so far from my cries of anguish? My God, I cry out by day, but you do not answer, by night, but I find no rest.* Matthew 27:46 About *three in the afternoon Jesus cried out in a loud voice Eli, Eli, lema sabachthani? (which means "MY God, my God, why have you forsaken me?)* I don't know about you but my closest times with the Lord have been in my storms. My prayers come from nothing but the heart to the mouth, LORD, HELP ME, PLEASE, and he always did.

When you start on these programs, you are told that they are not easy and that they are meant to break you and put you back together again. That made sense to me, but I didn't allow the program to break me, because after the first three months I turned off to the teaching and stopped listening. Instead, I would think of women and of my future partner. I wasn't in any state to hold down a marriage, but in my head I thought if I met a woman who would become my wife, then that would have the power to heal all the sickness inside me. Now today I know that to be lies, because I found out that it is the blood of Jesus that brings healing on the inside. That gift of healing was all because of Jesus' death on the cross.

I was one week into the program and had no intention of going back to Coatbridge to live. In fact, while I was at The Haven in the middle of nowhere, I didn't even want to see anyone from that way. Once I went out for a wee walk near The Haven, and I saw a white van drive up next to me. I looked through the window and saw a mate from Coatbridge in the van, coming for an interview. I couldn't believe it. The Haven is honestly quite a distance from Coatbridge and is quite remote, and there was an old mate I used to take drugs with. I was thinking, "Lord, give me peace. The Coatbridge ones are everywhere I go." This mate told me there was a Teen Challenge outreach bus in Coatbridge to help those with addiction to get away and learn how to know Jesus. I just had to see the funny side of it.

He left after two or three months of the program, and shortly after that ended up in prison.

Before going to The Haven, I had gone to a small Christian café' so I could get into The Haven. There was a Christian band there and a lot of addicts. I wasn't sure who the speaker was, as he seemed as mad as us, but all the sick people loved this man. His name was Roy Lees. Roy was also born and raised in Coatbridge and found God in prison after reading the book, **The Cross and the Switchblade**. Roy was married to a Christian woman named Mary. This was before he got put in prison for a few years. Mary would send Roy verses from the Bible, but he wasn't interested. All he ever wanted out of life was to be a millionaire. It was Roy's love of money that got him put in prison, and while he was doing his sentence he picked up this book, not realizing that God was going to change his life through it. In the book, David Wilkerson said to one of the gang leaders, "If you cut me into a thousand little pieces, every part of me will say I love you." After Roy read that, God's Holy Spirit touched him in a supernatural way and changed his life. After prison, Roy and his wife's cousin, David Black, started up The Haven. God has used David Black's family in a massive way to reach out for God's lost sheep (lost people).

My aim at The Haven should have been to get real with God, but at twenty-three I still wanted to do my own thing, and that was to chase women and still do the will of God. Trust me, it doesn't work! I wasn't listening to the word of God speaking into my life. All I was thinking of was sex. After nearly six months in The Haven, I had a day out, and the first thing I did was ask the guy who came and got me to drop me off at a woman's home near Coatbridge. You see, I knew she wasn't a Christian, and I knew I could get sex off her. So

I got to her home, got let in and there she was, lying in the bed. It was too good to be true. The only problem was that I claimed to be born again.

I was addicted to this sin; I had become obsessed with sex. I had transferred the obsession for heroin to sex. I honestly couldn't experience God's fullness because I was back in the darkness. Satan had got a grip on my life and he was telling me to ditch the Christian life because it wasn't real. I left the woman's house, knowing that what I had done was wrong in the eyes of God. I looked totally different from the outside, but I was still a mess on the inside. I was going to church and not even listening to the preaching. I was always hoping to meet my future wife and then I thought I could change. I was still very angry. I had not let The Haven break me to get rid of all this anger, so I was still a total mess inside. Only God could free me from this sin.

More Coatbridge people came and went. What Teen Challenge and The Haven were doing was great, but I always chose to do things my way instead of theirs. That's what always got me into trouble — doing things Paul's way.

I was on Phase Three and I met a woman at church. She wasn't a Christian, but she liked me and gave me her number. We got in touch by phone and wanted to meet up, but I was still in the program. We arranged that she would drive up at night and I would sneak out when everyone was in bed, then we would have sex in her car. After that, I would sneak back into The Haven.

Everything I was doing was wrong. I didn't even believe the whole Bible. I was blind to my own sins. I would never have got away with all this in Teen Challenge, as it was stricter. God knew what I was doing; there was no hiding the sin forever. God's plan for my life was for me to think of others and take them out of their sin. It wasn't for me to do all the things of the flesh, say sorry to God, and then it would be okay.

In The Haven we were up at 7:15am, to get dressed and clean and tidy our rooms, and have a quiet time at 7:45 before breakfast at 8 o'clock. Then it was clean-up duties and then church. Class study was at 10am, then lunch. After lunch, we had work duties, then dinner and then another class study. This was to help us put a structure in our lives. At night, before we went to our rooms at 10pm, we all spent fifteen minutes with the Lord. Ten men who had been involved in all kinds of crime were led in singing by wee Donny Black, David Black's younger brother, and we would all sing before bed, "Jesus loves me, this I know, for the Bible tells me so." It was all about doing things God's way, not my way.

As I'm writing this the date is 9-4-2015. I went into The Haven on 9-4-2004. Eleven years ago exactly. Maybe God has a reason for that.

When I got clean, I started to want porn; it was the addict in me. I had never really bothered with porn until I became a Christian. But you see, addicts love the build-up. It was like getting the heroin through the letter-box, go to a wee, secret place where you are alone, get the hit, but then it wasn't that good after all. For me, it was the same with porn and sex. I loved the build-up more than the acting out.

There were two sides to me. One side wanted to love everyone and please God, always do God's will, and speak the truth to all people. And then there was the other side of me, which wanted the selfish things to give me instant pleasure, and all the time I was searching for this instant pleasure. As a Christian, all I was doing was giving the devil more of a foothold in my life. The devil comes to steal, kill, and destroy, and I was giving him the opportunity to do it. I honestly believe that Christians have to be more educated about the addiction of sex. Most guys who leave Teen Challenge and fall back into addiction are going out to get a woman. There is definitely a serious problem to be dealt with.

PHASE FOUR

The only thing I did right in The Haven was not picking up drugs and drink, but there is only so long you can carry on in this sin without picking up drugs again. I still believed that humans came from apes, and by now I was on Phase Four. On this phase we had more freedom to come and go. My way of thinking was a mess. I was clean, but still had the head of an addict. You see, David Black and his wife had opened up the home for Phase Four, and Roy Lees' wife had become manager of The Haven. And they knew what I was up to.

In Phase Four, a church in Coatbridge (Whifflet) had asked me to give my testimony. The Christian band that had played in Port Glasgow at Roy's cafe was there playing, and most of my family were there to hear me, along with friends I had previously used drugs with, including Paddy, who I had grown up with. An hour before going to this church in Whifflet, I went to a woman's house, had sex with her, then went to my Mum's and got a taxi to the church, where everyone was waiting on me to tell them how much my life had changed around and to tell them about God. The whole church was full, waiting to hear me testify. I have to see the funny side of it now.

I walked into the church and started to walk to the front to speak, and as I walked the people stood up and started clapping their hands, as if I deserved their applause. I had just had sex an hour before. I felt like the worst man alive. I gave my testimony, but I didn't want to go on as if I'd done great. I kept it short. I had to. I was in sexual sin. Imagine if they knew what I had just done. Don't get me wrong. If people didn't understand about God and sin, they might not realize that it was wrong, but as a Christian, I knew it didn't please God.

After I had done my testimony at Whifflet Church, a guy called Robert came up to me and asked me where I was going to live after The Haven. He said I could get one of his flats, which happened to be in the same town and area as that G12 church I had been at. But after being offered this flat, I wondered how God could give me a blessing of this flat just after I had sex with a woman who was a friend of mine, and then gave my testimony about how God had changed my life. It honestly seemed really strange.

At the Haven, three other guys were with me in the room I shared with Willie. Two of the other guys were Protestants, Rangers supporters. I had been a Catholic and a Celtic fan. The other two began making fun of Catholics and Celtic supporters. Previously, I would have been offended and stuck up for the Catholic side, but instead I got up, walked out of the room, and sat outside. I didn't want all that stuff still in my life, because I knew how it had damaged me and messed with my way of thinking. I was still not well with the sickness of addiction. God had taken me to The Haven to learn a new way of living. The teaching I was getting and the way the program worked would have washed a lot of the old ways away, and if I had listened to God, it would have become more real, but I had turned off my listening.

G12 CHURCH

I went with a couple of guys from Port Glasgow to the G12 church. We had been sitting down for a while, then the two guys with me decided that they wanted to leave. At the end of the service, the same man who had previously spoken about his past, as if he was deep into drug addiction and drug dealing, wanted me to join his cell group. It didn't take long for me to see that he had some resentment towards me, not because I had done anything wrong or anything like that. I realized this guy was going to be hard work. I can only remember one guy from that cell group, and he also had had a problem with drugs in his past. The two of us honestly found the cell leader's testimony quite hard to believe.

I had been thrown out of The Haven because of my lust for women, and I still wanted to have sex outside God's will. Mary, the manager of The Haven, gave me chances to surrender my will to God and stop all this problem with lust and chasing women, but again I didn't take the advice seriously. Even knowing how dangerous all this was to me and my life, I just kept on going back to it and this problem just never left me. Even years later it still became a big problem in my life and when I wanted to serve Jesus it still became my most dangerous SIN, along with un-forgiveness and resentment. I was obsessed with sex; it was more powerful than heroin and other drugs.

I met a woman from Coatbridge who was attracted to me and she also had an attractive body. I knew this woman wasn't the one God wanted me to marry. She went to church with me and enjoyed the service.

As I walked in through the gates of the G12 church, I strongly felt a heaviness push down on me. My leader really got on my nerves with the way he would go about as a leader. He wanted to tell us to jump and he would have loved us to ask how high. It seemed as if some liked to control and insult others. There was another guy in that church who must have had a hatred for me, because at times he would look at me and I could see in his eyes that he didn't like me one bit. I must have said something about him when I was at that same church as an addict.

My leader and this other guy were the type of guys who had never been in a fight in their lives. You see, in these churches the leaders don't actually have to fight you to abuse you. The leaders of the G12 church were above everybody else — whatever they said to the pastor went — there wasn't another side to the story. The pastor and two other leaders had G12 registration plates on their cars. To them, this G12 vision was above all other visions, and, no matter what anyone said about it, they would think they were the ones being attacked.

I finished with the woman after three months, as I knew it wasn't from God, although she wasn't happy about it. Our church went for the weekend to Newcastle in England to see and hear the main man of the G12 speak. We got back on Saturday night and I didn't seem to be any different. You see, I was blind, with the devil telling me that the Bible wasn't true. I knew Satan had blinded me. On Sunday afternoon at church, I was seeking God's healing from the lie of evolution being real, and from the power of lust, which I couldn't control. The pastor was preaching, but it was God speaking to me through it, so I went to the front of the church for healing. The pastor put his hand on my head and I fell to the ground. I couldn't stop crying and I knew God had freed me from the lies of the devil telling me that God wasn't real. I had a supernatural experience. It was a conviction of all my past sin. I could see what I had put my family through. My family had been heartbroken with me and the way I lived my life. God showed me my family's pain over my sin.

God forgave me all my past sins. I got up and everything looked clean and new. I felt free and forgiven. I remembered that guy who had been touched by God when I was an addict, the guy who had been touched by God when he got out of prison, and I had always wanted a touch like that. It happened at the same place. God is good.

For a few days after that, I just prayed to God and read my Bible, scared to leave the comfort I was in. But pride got in on Friday. I stopped praying and went to meet the woman I had just finished with. However, she wanted to go down south to live. After that experience in church, she phoned me and told me that she had caught Hepatitis C from me and she had started the treatment to get rid of it, then she just hung up on me. It was like a punch to the stomach. I was sure that Hepatitis C was caught from sharing dirty needles and not really through sex. One of the men in that church talked to me about it after I told him about the phone call. He told me he was married and had a child when he had Hepatitis C, and he thought the hospital wouldn't have put that woman on that treatment so soon. It seems she had been telling lies to get back at me for finishing with her.

After I got touched by God, I knew God wanted me to go into Coatbridge and Airdrie and let people know what the good Lord can do for those who seek Him. I wanted to tell them that they didn't have to live that way, and to let them know more about salvation. I didn't just want them to know about Christian churches, I also wanted to tell them about Teen Challenge. My leader drove me there and I would go and see the drug addicts I knew to ask if they wanted to come to church with me, and then we would drive them there and then back again. A lot of people would come with us. These were the people God wanted: addicts, alcoholics, the sick, the lost. You see, they knew their lives weren't right and that they were sinners. It wasn't just on a Sunday they would come. They also came to the cell groups on Tuesday. In addition, on Thursday there were meetings to train us up to be cell leaders. The teaching was really good, but even so I never felt as free as I would have liked at church. There was just something not right about this vision they wanted everyone to follow.

I was always trying to seek God's kingdom. I thought that meant things I could see with my eyes, but God was talking about doing an inside job in my life. I hadn't really listened to the teaching in The Haven Christian rehabilitation center, and I still wasn't well, even though God was using me. I had done years of damage to myself with all the drug abuse. I had loads of energy in me and I couldn't just sit in the house; I had to be out walking. I didn't know that what I was suffering from was paranoia. I would walk into the town center and it felt as if all eyes were on me, and when cars drove past I thought they were talking about me. I thought that if God gave me a partner, everything would be so much better. I couldn't even hold a job down, never mind a marriage. I couldn't have supported a wife and family.

I had to get my past sickness dealt with first. I didn't even know what was wrong with me. I was obsessed with porn and acting out (masturbating). The addict was still part of my life. I had just changed from heroin to porn. I used to go to a dealer's home, pay for my bag of heroin and find a little secret place to have a hit. All that for one bag! So then I would be disappointed. It was the same with sex addiction. I would get a porn movie, put it in my jacket, and run home to watch it. Then after the build-up I would feel disappointed in myself, repent to God, and not want to do it again, but then see myself doing the same thing all over again.

I had all this anger inside me. I should have dealt with all that in The Haven by allowing the program to break me, but I hadn't, so this was the consequence of my disobedience. I always knew that God had been looking after me for His purpose, but I struggled to rest in God's love for me. I allowed Satan to cripple me with false guilt (condemnation). Satan is a very good liar. God wasn't angry with me; He loved me with unconditional love. I didn't need to earn that love. I felt so let down with some Christians and the church I was in. I could see that it was for the praise of man rather than God. When someone brought people to church, they would have them stand next to the person who brought them, like a trophy.

When people left that church, a lot of them went back to the church the pastor started off in, or a church in Glasgow. The leaders thought this was the work of Satan, but it was God taking them out of the G12 cult. This same church I went to had started off really well, then as it grew Satan saw pride in them. Even though they had invited the G12 vision into the church, they meant well. I found it hard to believe that the pastor of the church couldn't see that this vision was controlling and hurting many people. To me, it was as clear as day that they had made a big mistake. The pastor had a great love for the addicts and many other people, but it seemed he was blind to the real issue. Most of the leaders were really good at explaining the Bible. They attended church a lot, prayed and fasted and gave ten percent of their income, but the church was full of problems.

In G12, the pastor would have twelve leaders underneath him and each of those twelve would have a group they called a cell group, and everyone in the groups would try to get others into the group and to go to this same church. And then the ones in the group were supposed the leave the cell group after the training in the church on a Thursday night and start their own cell groups. It was all about numbers, and when you took them to church it was all about you bringing them there, rather than giving thanks to God and being humble. But instead of putting others before you, it looked in the church more about you getting a pat on the back for bringing them to church or the cell groups. The church had pride issues. The ones that never left the G12 church were all usually the ones related to the pastor in some way. It was like if you were outside this circle. The others had so much more power over you and if they didn't like you, they would make sure you felt their resentment.

There was one G12 leader who loved to attack the minds of the other believers in the church by being very flashy with his money, his job, his past profession. He even used his wife to say to other Christians who didn't have as much as him, "Ha ha, look what I've got and you haven't." It was clear that he loved the power it gave him. Can I tell you, the people who know Christ, I want to know the believers who know how to rejoice in storms, the born again believers who love the Lord during attacks from the enemy and the ones who let the Lord break them and turn them into soldiers of

God's army. The church wasn't all bad, there were a lot of loving and caring people there who honestly did love the Lord. People went into this vision not realizing how spiritually abused it could leave them afterwards.

To explain the things being taught in that church, I'll go over the routine of the G12 in one week there. Sunday we would go to church and bring as many people to it as we could. If we had people there with us, we would all stand next to our leader who led the cell group. Sometimes the pastor and the church would all clap their hands if you brought people to the church with you. Tuesday we would go to the cell leader's house where he or she (depending if your leader was male or female, my leader was male) would teach us all over again the message we got at church that Sunday. Thursday we would go to church to be trained as cell leaders, so one day we could have our own cell group.

To join a group, you would meet at church on Sunday. One of the leaders would come over to you and then he would take you aside and ask if you wanted to join his or her cell group. To be honest, the people who began to join the cell groups were moving about all the time to different groups and different leaders. A big aim these leaders had was to get as many people as they could to join their cell groups. It was clear that some of the leaders wanted their cell with many people attending to make them feel good about themselves. Pride and ego problems, this church had.

It seemed like a cult because the cell groups would all be split into different little groups all over the town, or villages just outside the town. If anyone left the church and cell groups and spoke about the vision being wrong, they would put a little smile on their faces and act as if they were the victims of the attacks from the enemy, coming through the ones who spoke against them and G12. They would not listen to anyone who had been hurt by certain leaders. You see, most of them were related to the pastor, so your word didn't mean anything to him and certain leaders knew that and played on it.

People seemed to fall for it because it was enticing. I can speak about when I was there. I knew all this was all wrong and not from God. I knew I wanted out of the place, but it was like if I left it God would be angry with me and his blessings would all stop in my life. People were leaving it and saying the same thing: they felt really hurt and let down by the way they were treated by certain leaders. The enemy is behind this vision and the enemy has been telling many people all over the world about this being from God, so it can leave us believers hurt and wounded by it all. People did believe the lies at the beginning and may have left to follow Christ.

I always had someone in addiction staying in my flat. I would tell them about Teen Challenge and about how God changes people's lives. I didn't preach. I left that to the pastor. I always kept it real. I was always put off by Christians who got too heavy into the Bible, and I was more attracted to Christians who kept it real, so that was the way I tried to help others. At this time I had a religious way of doing things, always trying to bring to salvation everyone I spoke to. I would be telling people about God when I was getting a haircut, talking about God as I sat next to someone on the bus. Everyone I spoke to, I would tell them about God.

I always wanted to stay pure and clean before the Lord. There were certain areas of my walk with God that had to be cleaned up. 2 Timothy chapter 2 verse 22 says, 'Flee the evil desires of youth and pursue righteousness, faith, love and peace along with those who call on the Lord out of a pure heart.'

God wanted me to go back to Coatbridge and Airdrie and tell the addicts I knew that the God of the Bible loved them and wanted to free them from their slavery to drugs and drink. One day in Greenend, I had noticed an old friend of mine, Paddy, who used to go about with my older cousin. I had stolen five pounds from his Mum when I was a kid. Paddy told me that the doctor had just stopped his Methadone. Paddy started going to church with me and also going to the Teen Challenge bus that sat in Coatbridge, and he was thinking of going into The Haven for rehab. Paddy's and my leader said Paddy didn't need a Christian rehab center. All he needed to do was go to church with us and attend his cell group, but I knew God wanted Paddy to get away to a program. Paddy stayed at my home a lot to get away from Greenend and to learn about Jesus.

When I went to The Haven, I didn't let the program break me and put me back together again. Now, when I was in my flat on my own, I expressed my anger to God. I was full of deep anger inside me, and because I allowed certain Christians to walk all over me, I felt let down by God, so I would blame God for it. I would say to God, "How come he's getting all this material stuff and I'm not?" It was as if I was telling God I deserved it more than the other person. That was the pride inside me. Deep down inside me, if I was honest I just knew I wasn't ready for a lot of God's blessings yet.

I was very insecure at that time, and I would tell people in the church too much information about myself, which was not a good idea. I was just giving them ammunition to use against me. I was looking for answers about the Bible and the nature of God and salvation. I had all these obsessions in me that needed to be removed by the Holy Spirit, but I didn't understand that then.

God could have said to me, 'How dare you feel guilty for the sins of your past? My Son Jesus has taken your guilt and punishment by dying on the cross." I was walking about with false guilt. The Bible tells us there is no condemnation for those who are in Christ. I had to learn to shake off the devil's lies.

PADDY AT THE HAVEN

Paddy entered The Haven on 27th February, 2006. My landlord took Paddy and me to The Haven for his first day. Paddy was out of his face on heroin and he was like a fish out of water at the beginning of the program. That's what it was like for most of us. The first week he was there he was wondering why he had given up his home to go there.

When you come to know Jesus and read the Bible, what you learn is very different from the way Paddy and I were brought up to believe. The Bible says we are to forgive our enemies, and even to love our enemies. Now, that is alien to most people. When Paddy decided to let the program do what it could for him, God started to do His inside work in Paddy's life.

Have you ever been in that place where you realize that everything you've done has done you harm, and then you decide to do it God's way? Well, that's what it's like for most of us when we go into Teen Challenge programs. A lot of people don't go in to meet with God, but then they do. Paddy had to learn a lot of new teachings. He had to let go and let God do what He wanted in his life. On his first day at The Haven, one of the staff members commented that Paddy wouldn't last a week, but at the end of the program, that same staff member was the one chosen to give Paddy his certificate. By the end of Paddy's program, they said he was one of the best students they had ever had.

Even though I struggled in the church I was in, I still had a great experience with God. I was at this church for about three years. The last few months I was there, the pastor was sure that God was telling him to go to Glasgow and start a church there that would hold two thousand seats. Glasgow is known for having the worst crime rate of any city in Britain, and this church was planning to go in with their G12 vision and help it. Well, they believed that was what God wanted, so they went with all guns blazing.

At the same time, a guy who had done a Teen Challenge program came to live with me. Before I met him, he had prayed for a wife, and everything he asked for, God had given him. He thought he was ready to hold down a marriage. They were married after a year's relationship, and then everything that he hadn't dealt with came up. His best mate got shot dead and this guy was broke, so he picked up drugs and drink again. He started going to A.A. meetings and there they spoke about the sickness.

He told me that in some Christian circles, A.A. and the 12 steps were like a bad word, even though it is the God of the Bible who started the A.A., not to preach but to help people get well. The two of us had to get educated about what we were suffering from. When this guy was married, he had a beautiful wife, a good job, and a nice car, and he would ask God, "What's wrong with me?" I was the same. You see, I hadn't done the program the way it was meant to be done, so these were the consequences.

Even when I was attending church, that's when God led me into A.A. to get a clear understanding of what I was suffering from, and that was the sickness of drugs and alcohol. When I wasn't at church, I would go to the meeting and listen to what the people were talking of when they spoke about their way of thinking when on drink and how they managed to get well after the alcohol. And I went back to the same church when I wasn't attending A.A. meetings. At the same time, I felt really wounded inside by church and no real understanding of my sickness of past addictions. At the same time, I was enjoying the recovery from A.A. At the same time, I could feel in my spirit that God was taking me out of G12.

I knew this one guy who said that he and his Dad were told to leave the cell group because they weren't fruitful. Being fruitful in the cell group means bringing people to the Lord or being changed by God in the cell group. The leader was saying he couldn't see anything good come out of the father and son. Galatians 5 :22-23 *But the fruit of the Spirit is Love, joy, peace, forbearance, kindness, goodness, faithfulness, gentleness, and self-control.* And such things there is no law. I wanted to get out of my leader's cell and start my own. So I suggested to this man that I could start my own group, and he and his father could come to it. I walked into the church to tell the pastor about it, but he wasn't one bit happy with the plan. In fact, he said I was wrong to criticize the first cell leader for telling the two guys to leave the group because they weren't fruitful. I walked out of the church and God showed me a vision in the Spirit of the G12 vision, and God said it was not from Him.

I started going to a church in Glasgow, and this church knew about the church I had left, because others were there who had gone through and done the same things I had. I found that this church was doing a recovery course of 12 steps, and I was interested in this because I knew I had to do a lot of inside work on myself. The

12 steps program is a gift from God. It lets you understand that God can show you areas of your life that can make you not well, and how God can give you the tools to get rid of the areas that are in some way making you not well. I still didn't realize I was as sick as I was. The good news is that Jesus came for the sick.

    I spent a few weeks at this church, but then I started thinking that I had to go back to the G12 church to please God, even though God had told me to get out of it. I listened to unclean spirits that wanted me back at that church. I went back thinking and hoping God wanted to bless me, even though I knew it was wrong. I needed God to get rid of this spiritual abuse that was in my life. God didn't want me back there. The crazy thing about all this was that I couldn't understand how the pastor of this church couldn't see all this as being wrong. Despite all the problems, he was a good man with a good heart.

WALKING OUT OF THE WILL OF GOD

I had an argument with a man who was sleeping in my flat for a few days. This same man said he wanted into a Teen Challenge to get help, so I decided to go out a walk to the town center, and on the way I told God I didn't need Him. My plan was to see a woman who liked me, so I went to the town center hoping to meet her. As I was walking past a shop, I noticed a young woman packing a shelf in a shop and I went over to her and asked her for her number. I also asked her age and she told me she was nineteen. She got her phone and gave me her number, then started to walk further into the store, so I walked behind her. She turned round and I asked her for a kiss, so she kissed me. Then I put my hand on her chest, not up her top. It was for about three seconds. Then I noticed a man walking in front of me, so I stopped kissing her. I walked out of the shop, thinking nothing of it.

A few weeks earlier, God had told me to surrender all to Him (porn, acting out). I stopped doing that, but had still left doors open for Satan to get in. After kissing the young woman, I went to a supermarket to get food for that day, but before I went home, I walked by the same shop where the young woman worked. A police officer was

Redemption through the blood

standing at the shop door, and as I went past he walked over and grabbed me. At first I thought they were thinking I had shop-lifted, but I soon realized that the young woman had told lies. She had told the other woman in the shop and the police that I had grabbed her, patted her back and her bum, told her she better kiss me, and then put my hand up her top and bruised her chest. I was thinking there was no way the police or court would believe that.

I got in the police car and was taken to the police station, expecting that after hearing my story, they would know the woman was telling lies. They put me in a cell and eventually I was interviewed by two officers. I told them exactly what had happened. They must have thought I was a religious nut-case. I was talking about not having a TV* because God had told me to get rid of it, and that I had stopped masturbating. I just thought that by telling them the truth, they would believe me. How wrong I was.

*(I was in church and I heard in my spirit God saying to me to get rid of my TV, so I asked the guy next to me if he would take me to my flat so I could get rid of my TV. He agreed, and as we were walking out of the church to do it, a guy from the band waved me over so he could ask me if I wanted his guitar. Of course I did! So after that, I believed God had given me the guitar for getting rid of the TV. The guy from the band didn't know I had just given away my TV. The next day I was sitting on my chair with the guitar, wondering how to tune it. (Imagine if I had told the police all this — they would have thought I was totally off my head.) As I was sitting with the guitar, I could hear someone playing a guitar downstairs from me. I went down the stairs and told this guy, who had recently moved in, that I had just got a guitar and I asked him if he would tune it for me. He also very kindly gave me papers on how to play it.)

The next day I had to appear at the Sheriff Court. I was still thinking all I needed to do was speak to the judge without my lawyer and the judge would give me a wee slap on the back of the hand and let me out. I was put in a cell with one other guy, away from the other cells. The officers in the court opened the hatch and told me my lawyer wanted to speak with me. I asked the lawyer what he expected to happen and he told me that I would go to prison. I got a fright! I wasn't scared of prison, but I was scared to go to prison as a man who had been done for sexual assault. I went back to my cell and I prayed to God that if He would get me out of this mess, I would never again do anything like act out, porn or sex. As I was praying, the hatch was opened and the officer told me I was free to go. The Procurator Fiscal couldn't find anything on me. I got out, laughing about it.

One of the guys who were staying with me was waiting outside the court. On the bus, we were laughing and joking about it. It didn't take me long to forget all about it. The two men staying with me moved on. I met up with Lisa, an old friend I used to use drugs with. She was a Catholic and had really good faith in Jesus. A guy I knew had just finished a Teen Challenge program at a place called Duns, in Scotland. He asked me if I wanted to go to an Overcomers Outreach in Glasgow. It included the 12 steps and was all Christian-based. I remember Lisa and I going to the meeting together, and we enjoyed it. I'm not sure whether Lisa was using heroin a lot at that time, but I know she also had a lot of work to do on herself. She had been brought up in a good family and was pretty intelligent.

Someone I knew told me about a Christian homeless unit in the east end of Glasgow, and that they were looking for workers. I got their number and had an interview. A mate of mine was staying at my home until he got a place on a Teen Challenge program, and the two of us helped at this homeless center. It went well for me. I got two days shift to begin with, once they had done a disclosure, and my mate soon got his place on the Teen Challenge program.

Almost two months from the time I got arrested, I was reading the Bible from Hebrews chapter 12, and the Holy Spirit touched me as I was reading. I mentioned it to Paddy as I was talking to him on the phone, and he told me that he was doing work on Hebrews chapter 12 too. Paddy was on the staff at The Haven. I knew God was speaking to me on that chapter and the verses that caught my eye were verses 5 and 6:

"My son, do not make light of the Lord's discipline, and do not lose heart when he rebukes you, because the Lord disciplines those he loves, and he punishes everyone He accepts as a son."

The next day after the interview in Glasgow about the job in the homeless unit, I was praying to God when there was a knock at my door. The postman handed me a large letter. It was from the Sheriff's Court, about the woman I had kissed. All I could do was take it to my lawyer. As I was heading to his office, I felt as if this charge was really opening me up and I felt powerless. When I met my lawyer at the Sheriff's Court, he told me he'd sort it. After that I felt a bit more peace about it. My head was still done in with the charge hanging over me. My lawyer told me I could go to jail for this and it terrified me that I could be jailed as a sex offender. I knew I would have known people in the jail, and what could I have said to them? As far as I knew, the people from my past would have thought there was no way I would have been back in jail, especially for a charge like that. I had never lifted my hand to a woman in my life, but here I was with this charge saying I had bruised a seventeen-year-old's chest. Even though she told me she was nineteen, she happened to be seventeen.

I knew the only one who could get me out of this mess was God. God knew the truth of it all. If I went back to drugs and alcohol, then the Bible says that seven demons would enter back into my life and that would make things even worse than before. But one day while I was out walking, with my head all over the place, there must have been an unclean spirit speaking to me about ending my own life, and what I did was ask Satan to make me end my life. I don't think it was from my own mind, but I believe it was the devil. The minute I had done that, I couldn't believe what I had just done. What could go wrong did go wrong.

Just after that, I was in two Sunday papers. The report didn't say much about it, but it gave my name and address. I wondered what everyone would think of me. Then I got a call from a doctor in Monklands Hospital, asking whether I wanted to go on the Hepatitis C treatment, which makes you feel suicidal and paranoid. Because of sharing dirty needles, I caught Hepatitis c (hep c), at seventeen. As I mentioned further back in the story, when that women I was with said she had got it off me, she was telling lies as it's a disease you catch with sharing needles. Plus it takes up to six months to show in your blood, plus the doctors wouldn't put her on the treatment so soon, I mean I was with her for three months. The enemy knows what that treatment was like and it's a poison that fights against the Hepatitis c to get rid of it. It's not an easy treatment to go through. So I just went on the treatment and it made this charge seem about ten times worse. My name was in the Sunday paper, and on Monday I went to the Overcomers meeting. As I was walking through the town center, I saw this man I knew from the meetings, so I told him what had happened. He started saying, "What are you like kissing a girl in a shop…" then he started sticking his finger at the side of my head. This just made things worse. It gave me self-hatred for letting him do that to me. This was the work of the devil, to get me sicker. I didn't know what to think.

Round about this time in my life, God started speaking to me from the book of Exodus about how He had taken the Jews out of slavery and headed them towards the Promised Land.

God wanted me at that meeting. I knew I had to be there even though that man would also be there. This wasn't the first Christian I had met who played with Christians' minds. They are the ones Satan loves to use. I asked Satan to help me end my life and he started using the sickest of Christians. I was in a dark place at this time and I was broken. I was looking for a sponsor, someone who could educate me about this sickness I had. I was still recovering from past drug abuse.

I wanted to do the 12 steps. I had started attending a church in Glasgow that ran a recovery group, led by ex-addicts. I had just started my Hepatitis C treatment, and I took it really bad. I knew I would meet people in prison who I had known before. The devil was attacking me from every angle. This treatment was making me very aggressive. I had a lot of underlying anger and Satan kept reminding me of certain people who had treated me unfairly. I was really angry with God and I would blame God for all this. Remember, it wasn't God, but I had been let down by so many Christian leaders, the ones who had a bit of power and used it against people.

I met a man called Peter in Overcomers. It was Peter who had birthed Overcomers in a certain part of Glasgow. He had done a lot of inside work on himself and I wanted his teaching. Peter and I went to the church to do 12 steps, and he became my sponsor. The only way I could get all this mess in my life to end was through God. When I was being taught by Peter, he told me he had been sexually abused when he was a kid, and through the abuse became a sex addict. Peter got touched by God in the early 1970s. He said that the first six months of knowing God were the best six months of his life, until he met a Christian who said Peter surely had felt the wrath of God. Peter insisted it was the love of God he had known.

Then he began to go to a church called Children of God, and that was a cult. Peter taught me that I wasn't alone in all the sickness I had been through. I needed to understand what I was suffering from. At the beginning of our lives as Christians, the two of us were full of religion. We had deep wounds to deal with. He had already done a good few years of work on himself through Alcoholics Anonymous, Narcotics Anonymous, and Sexaholics Anonymous, and even after slipping back into his addictions he got back on track in 2001 and returned to N. A. meetings, and began praying again to Jesus.

I left the church in Glasgow. I was going through the Spiritual Journey 12 steps book that Peter had taken me through. That had been a painful course, because God had used it to get rid of a lot of my underlying anger. I had been expressing a lot of this anger at God because I couldn't forgive the Christians who had walked all over me. During the first few years of my walk with the Lord, I was broken, and bullies could see that and seemed to enjoy using their power over me.

The court case kept being put back because they needed more evidence. I went to another church after being on the Hepatitis C treatment for a few months. The church service was on Malachi chapter 3 verses 6-10.

"I the Lord do not change. So you, O descendants of Jacob, are not destroyed. Ever since the time of your forefathers you have turned away from my decrees and have not kept them. Return to me and I will return to you," says the Lord Almighty.
But you ask,"How are we to return?"
"Will a man rob God? Yet you rob me."
But you ask."How do we rob you?"
"In tithes and offerings. You are under a curse–the whole nation of you–because you are robbing me. Bring the whole tithe into the storehouse that there may be food in my house. Test me in this," says the Lord Almighty, "and see if I will not throw open the floodgates of heaven and pour out so much blessing that you will not have room enough for it."

God was saying to me that if I surrendered my sins to Him (acting out and porn), He would throw open the floodgates of heaven. If I did my bit, He would do His. I left the church full of the Holy Spirit. A lot of the fear had left me and I felt more at peace. I actually enjoyed the challenge. All that week, I tried to stay focused on God. The following Sunday, I went to the same church, feeling really down and depressed. When I got to church, guess what, it was on the same verses, Malachi 3 vs 6-10. That is the only time I have been to the same church with the same teaching as the week before.

I wanted a comfort, and instead of staying pure before the Lord and getting through that one night, I went out from my flat and ran to a shop to buy a magazine with naked women, got home and disobeyed God's instructions. After that, I became addicted to acting out. Even though I knew what God had said, I refused to give up

Walking Out Of The Will Of God

this sexual sin. I honestly didn't feel as in tune with God. I knew God would bring this charge to an end if I had done my bit, but I hadn't.

At the end of the year, Paddy phoned me up to tell me I could go to Teen Challenge in London and work for four weeks. I agreed, thinking I would go to work as staff in Teen Challenge in London and it would be easy. How wrong was I! When I got there, I had been about four months on the Hepatitis C treatment and I had a charge hanging over me. Satan still had power over my life because I had asked him to help me end my life. My head was all over the place and I was trying to be a staff member in this program. I started coming out in spots all over my face with the stress.

I was reading the Bible, and the Holy Spirit touched me when I was reading about God moving His people to another land. Remember, God had already spoken to me about the Promised Land. Paddy phoned me about giving up my flat and moving to Port Glasgow into one of Davie's rented flats, and sharing it with a guy I knew well from Greenend. This guy had been into The Haven right after me.

The four weeks at Teen Challenge had ended and it hadn't been easy. The residents could tell I wasn't well, and the last thing I wanted was for them to know I had a charge hanging over me. Paddy and I got back to my flat as soon as we returned to Scotland and started packing my stuff into a van, so we could get to Davie's home in Kilmacolm. Davie is a man of God and we knew each other really well. Davie knew I had a problem of lust with women, and as it had been in two Sunday papers, Davie was pretty hard on me, thinking it was God bringing my sins to light. But it wasn't God. It was from the pit of hell, because I had given Satan power in my life. I spent four weeks in Kilmacolm at Davie's home. Davie and his wife, Jean had done nothing but help the sick and they showed such love to me. They opened their home to let the Phase Four guys finish their program there. They took me in because they knew I was going through a hard time. Davie was hard on me as he wasn't sure what had happened to me.

When I left their home, I went to share a flat with an old mate, Jamie. Davie had bought several homes and he rented some of them out to Teen Challenge residents who had moved on after their program. I finished the treatment I had been on in that flat. The Hepatitis C left my body and I was all clear of it. Bob, one of The Haven staff, went with me to court and the lawyer explained that if I pleaded guilty to the main charge, the judge would drop some of the minor charges, like patting her back and bum, even though I hadn't done that. But if I didn't plead guilty I would be guilty of it all, if I was found guilty. So I did the wrong thing and stopped trusting God for the truth to set me free. I panicked and pleaded guilty. So my lawyer went in to see the judge and for some strange reason Bob and I left the court, got in the car and headed back home.

The lawyer then phoned and asked why I had left. That was God looking after me. I believe I would have been put in jail if I had stayed at court, but God intervened. As I had pleaded guilty, I had to go to Greenock to see the probation officers and explain to them exactly what had happened. They wanted the full story so they could write it down and take it back to the judge for my next visit to court. I had been charged with something I hadn't done. I had asked the girl for a kiss, she had kissed me, I put my hand on her chest, but not up her top. A man had come by and we had stopped kissing. What I had been charged with was different. I couldn't sit there and tell them a story that I hadn't done. But through all this, God was doing some work in me.

In Kilmacolm, I was at Davie's prayer meeting, and as he was about to start he looked at me, and all I could see in his eyes was love. He looked straight at me and said, "Paul, this is for you; Romans chapter 8 verses 31-39." I couldn't wait to get back home to read it, as I knew it was from God to me. After the meeting, Paddy and I went back to his girlfriend's home and I started reading Romans ch.8 vs.31-39, and I couldn't stop laughing. Paddy asked me why I was laughing and I told him it was the Holy Spirit in me. I got a very strong feeling of the Spirit's presence, telling me it was all going to work out fine and that God was with me.

Romans ch. 8 vs. 31 starts off by saying that if God is with you, then who can be against you? When I was in my twenties, I was going through withdrawal and I couldn't sleep, so I put on a World War II movie and an American soldier said, "If God is with us, then who can be against us?" That verse had always stuck in my mind and now it was in my spirit.

HEALING ROOM, GREENOCK

I had been to the Healing Room in Greenock town center, and I had told them what I had said to Satan about allowing unclean spirits into my life to make me end my life. I had told them about my life following that, about the charge and the court. I went on my hands and knees and they put their hands on me and started praying for me. I couldn't stop crying, and Satan's hold on my life was broken. I felt like a new man, really refreshed, and the heavy feeling upon my life had been removed.

The morning I was due at the Sheriff's Court, I picked up my Bible. It was 25th March, so I decided to read Proverbs ch 25. I had marked all the Proverbs with a felt-tip pen and the only chapter that wasn't marked was Proverbs ch. 25. I knew God was telling me something. What stuck out to me was verses 4 and 5. "Remove the dross from the silver, and out comes material for the silversmith; remove the wicked from the king's presence, and his throne will be established through righteousness."

Bob went with me to the Sheriff's Court not long after that, and my lawyer told me I could get six months, nine months, or up to a year. We went in and the judge was reading the background reports. The Procurator Fiscal, a woman, was speaking about the charge and it was as if she was going to start crying. The judge knew that when I had spoken to the probation officers I had told them I hadn't done what I had been charged with. The judge looked at me and said my sentence would be one-and-a-half years on the sex offenders list and one-and-a-half years on probation. I didn't get put in prison because my God is bigger than all lies. Bob is what you would call a mighty man of God. In my darkest times, that man would always reach out to me, and it was as if he could feel my pain with me. Bob doesn't want anything from me except for me to know he loves and wants the best for me.

Paddy's younger brother, Tosh, had just finished at The Haven at this time and had met a woman from Coatbridge. Tosh had run about with me all our lives. He had been a hardcore addict, out every day to make ten pounds for a bag of heroin. Pride got into Tosh, the woman he had met ended the relationship, and Tosh started using again after three years of knowing God. He wasn't going to church or seeking God after The Haven. A storm came and he picked up drugs again.

I had a paper telling me where the Healing Rooms were in Scotland. One afternoon there was one somewhere in Glasgow, so I got the train to the main station and then had to find the train to take me to an area of Glasgow I knew nothing about. On that second train, I met a woman I recognized from the Healing Rooms in Greenock, and she was going to the same stop as me. I had a good feeling that God was directing me. We got off the train and the woman's daughter was picking her up, so they offered to take me to the church I was looking for, and they dropped me off there. I would never have found it by myself. I knew then that God wanted me there. I went into the church on my own, and as I was speaking to the two people who were there, a woman who was praying for me in a different room came in too. She felt she needed to come in and tell me I should stop being so religious and instead start to speak to the Holy Spirit as my friend. She also told me to read Isaiah ch 45, and to use my name, Paul, instead of the name Cyrus in the chapter. It is at times like this that you realize why you needn't worry about anything, because God has everything under His control.

BEFORE MY LAST COURT CASE

I was in the flat in Port Glasgow, praying to God as I walked around the table, when the Holy Spirit led me to my Bible, which was lying open on the table. I started to read Genesis ch 12, verses 1-3. The Holy Spirit's presence was so strong, I had to find out exactly what God was saying to me. A few days later, a friend of mine drove me to a church in Glasgow and I knew it was a spiritual Christian church. I went in the church and thought that if at the end of the service they asked if anyone wanted a healing, I would go to the front for healing, but guess what? The service was based on Genesis ch.12 vs. 1-3.

I kept going to the A.A. meetings in the area where I was staying, to get more understanding of the illness of addiction. I have great respect for 12 step programs, as my God gave them to us as a gift from Him. At these meetings, I met Catholics who were born again. God was showing me that what some Christians who told me that Catholics were not saved were telling lies. I don't believe some Christians who have said that God does not accept Catholics. I don't think they mean to tell lies, but what they say can be hurtful and untrue.

I was out walking in Port Glasgow, fasting and praying to God, and as I was praying, I met the same women from the Healing Room, and also the woman and daughter who had given me a lift to that church. When I met them, I heard God telling me to go to Glasgow and God would put a certain woman in my path. I got the train into Glasgow Central, turned right, and met the same woman God had told me to meet. I said hello and she asked me what I wanted. I tried speaking to her, but she told me to go back home. I couldn't tell her that God had told me to meet her there. That same woman was a woman I had met a couple of years after I left The Haven and had started to volunteer in Glasgow town center. I hadn't really fancied her, but I got obsessed with her before I started to get into recovery programs. Every time I was in Glasgow, I always wanted to meet her.

On this day after meeting her, I was saying to God that I had done what He told me to, even though I looked like an idiot. It was a thirty-minute train journey from where I was living. The woman probably thought I was off my head. It didn't make much sense then, but I knew God was a mysterious God.

I had found out that the G12 group that moved into Glasgow went back to the church they had been at before they moved away, as God hadn't blessed their work in Glasgow. When they left Glasgow, they realized that G12 was wrong and got rid of the vision. When I started going to Overcomers Outreach, Lisa was in my life. She had started going to the G12 church in Glasgow and had told the pastor that she believed it to be wrong. The pastor walked away and put it to an end. I met Lisa after that, and she had been off drugs for a year, walking with the Lord, and in the same church, which had changed.

I was in Greenock town center, and all of a sudden started thinking that I needed to be somewhere on my own and cry out to God. I was walking about but couldn't find anywhere quiet, so I decided to see if Davie's church was open so I could go in and pray. The church was closed, but across the road was another church, and the pastor was outside and up a ladder, painting it. I got talking to him and he invited me into the building to pray. I went to the front of the church and was praying as I walked to and fro, but I couldn't concentrate with the pastor sitting at the back of the church, watching me. I knelt down, closed my eyes and started speaking to God, and then I saw a vision of the addicts in Coatbridge and I couldn't stop crying. As I left the church, I knew God was there with me, showing me a picture of the hurting in my old town. I had no interest in going back to Coatbridge; in fact, I wanted to go abroad and help people in other countries.

Davie was doing up a one-bedroom flat for me to move into, and I was excited about this new flat he was giving me. I was one year in Port Glasgow when Davie told me someone else was going to move into that flat I thought I'd be getting. That person happened to be the guy who lived next door to the flat, so Davie gave him the flat he had been doing up and I moved into the one he had left, so we were next door neighbors. The flat I got was a total mess. I couldn't believe Davie would do something like that.

A pastor of David Wilkerson came down from New York with 200 of his church people. He had watched a film of The Haven, and David Black spoke about how hard it is helping all these people in and outside of The Haven. The pastor said that Scotland was going to have a revival. God is going to do something in Scotland because I believe it is a beautiful but hurting country. God is giving birth to a revival in Scotland.

I was listening to music while walking to Roy's church when God said to me that young men see visions and old men dream dreams. God showed me a vision of me injecting heroin while leaning against a church in Whifflet, Coatbridge. I used to take drugs at the back of a Christian church called Church of God. When I was an addict, I didn't even know this was a Christian church. God was sending me back to Coatbridge. I didn't tell anyone about this. Soon after this, my sister, who had seen the flat Davie had given me, told me to come back home. She didn't want me staying in a place like that. I had been in Port Glasgow for fourteen months. I thought Coatbridge must be the Promised Land I'd been waiting on. As I was walking to Roy's church in Port Glasgow, God told me that the Church of God in Coatbridge was going to be like Roy's, and there would be a band at the church and there would be sinners wanting to change.

When I had finished the 12 steps, I heard God say to me very clearly that if He hadn't taken my anger, then I would have taken it out on someone else. I believe I would have ended up snapping at someone and regretting it. I still had anger in me, but a lot had been removed. I was still refusing to forgive my enemies and was still resentful towards God for letting them do what they did. I know God had nothing to do with it, but I was shouting at God to get back at them for what they had done to me.

LOVE, SEX, MARRIAGE, PORN

*A*ll these were very powerful in my life. Controlling those feelings seemed so difficult to do. My walk with the Lord right now was far from perfect. I was single and attracted to the opposite sex. If I hadn't been a Christian and if I hadn't known right from wrong, I would have been out chasing women, or spending hours on the Internet chasing images of sex. If Jesus had been right there speaking to me and asking if I would like Him to remove my attraction for porn, I would have said, "Yes, Lord, remove." Each day I had to decide who I wanted to please, the spirit or the flesh. God had already told me why He hadn't taken it from me — because He wanted to use my weakness as my strength so it would glorify Him. A coach doesn't train an athlete only on their strong points, but a coach concentrates on the weak spots too. That's what God was doing for me, but it wasn't easy.

I always prayed for a partner, hoping God would bless me with a partner and then everything would go well. Deep down, I knew I wasn't ready to be a husband or a father. I used to pray every day for God to meet my needs. I would never have been able to hold down a marriage. I still had a lot of resentment in me, and if a woman had seen me shouting at God she would have freaked out.

COATBRIDGE

I was back at my Mum's house to do the will of God in my town, I knew nearly all of the addicts there, and the alcoholics, too, and I also knew God wanted me at the Church of God in Whifflet. It didn't take that long before God put people in my path. I started taking a good mate of mine to the church. Sammy had ended up in a wheelchair from obsessive drinking. He was always laughing and cracking jokes.

One day as I was sitting at my Mum's, an old friend of mine walked past. I went out and started speaking to her, telling her about the Teen Challenge bus that was parked in Whifflet near the train station, and she agreed to meet up with me and go to the bus. I didn't think she had any interest in God. We met up and went to the bus, and she really enjoyed her time there. She had been on heroin for a good number of years but was now on Methadone. There was a Ash path at the back of where we both lived, and we used to go to a field there to pray. One day we were out in the field and the two of us were speaking to God. As we were walking back home, she stopped very still because she experienced a touch from the Holy Spirit. She stood there, saying that she could feel God. I told her that when she got down on her Methadone she could go to Hope House, the Teen

Challenge center in Wales. She was looking forward to this. Her life was now in God's hands. She had told me that before she met me she was thinking of ending her own life.

Big Indoo (James) also came into my life. He also was fed up with his life, but he would turn up at the Teen Challenge bus and also go to church with me. Very soon I could see God at work in Coatbridge. I also met James, another mate of mine from when we were kids. He also had a heart for the Lord, but he struggled with addictions.

I was there for one reason, and that was to do the will of God. I hadn't had sex with a woman for four years. I was in the town center and I saw a woman I knew from my past. She wasn't a Christian. She asked me if I wanted to meet her that night, and I agreed. I knew I had the choice of not going up to her house to meet her. After we talked, I left her and went to my Mum's, knowing that if I went up to her house I'd end up having sex with her. I had been back in Coatbridge for two months and here I was faced with choosing to do the will of God and seeing people's lives being changed, or going up to her house and having sex with her. I knew God had put people in my life so I could lead them to the Lord. No one had to tell me it was wrong, but I decided to go up to the woman's home. We had sex, and afterward I wished I hadn't done that.

I was trying to be like Jesus and love the sick. You can't turn the clock back, but you can repent and change. After we did that, there was a tie between us. I enjoyed being in her company and we were good mates. But when you know Jesus, you know that you shouldn't be like the world because they don't know any different. I was meant to be in Coatbridge, but instead I was with a woman who loved the flesh.

The girl who I had helped earlier, who had been touched by the Holy Spirit in the field, had also met someone at the same time as me. I told her she shouldn't be going with that guy, even though at the same time I was out of the will of God in sexual sin. Not long after speaking to her about her relationship, and her stopping going to the Teen Challenge bus, I was going to church when the man she was seeing asked me if I had told her to stop seeing him. He was a decent man, but I could tell he was pretty violent. I just explained myself. I didn't want any violence in my life. I just wanted to get things right before God. Not long afterwards, the man she was seeing ended up in prison for about a year.

If I hadn't been a Christian and hadn't known God, I would have been having a great time. I knew what this stuff had done to me before with the charge. I was finishing my last six months on probation in Coatbridge, and I knew the mother of one of the probation officers was a social worker from my youth. I knew what I was doing, sleeping with this woman, was wrong. I would leave her telling her this was wrong, but she was thinking it was just a normal thing to have sex. She also liked the cocaine and alcohol. I was meant to be there in Coatbridge, helping people with these addictions. I felt the fear of God. I started getting bumps on the back of my head from this stress, and it was five years before they finally cleared up.

After about six months with her, I finally got a flat in between Airdrie and Coatbridge. After a couple of months, I got on my knees and asked God to take away the feelings I had for her. She had wanted to have a relationship with me but I knew it wasn't from God. I walked away from her a lot, but when I wasn't with her I was always wondering who else she was with. She was a bit of a party animal, and if I wouldn't go out with her, if she wanted to go with another guy,

I couldn't say anything. God removed from me the feelings I had for her. I was meant to be leading hurting people to the church God had called me to. My head was all over the place.

I was still not well with this unforgiveness, mostly two leaders from G12.

It was like poison to me. I knew the answer was to pray blessings over them, but I wouldn't. It left me not well, with my mind full of resentment. It was just not Jesus. If I prayed for my enemies, it did go away, but evil spirits would always remind me of the past. It shouldn't have been about whether God would bless my enemies. I should just have been praying so Satan couldn't mess with my head. They say that resentment is the number one offender. It's not good.

I wanted to rest in God's love for me — I honestly knew deep down how much He loved me. Some Christians get it straight away God's love. I always knew God loved me, and knowing the Lord's love even when things aren't going great for you. God's love doesn't go up and down; it's always the same love. God can't stop loving you. It's too good to be true. There are many hurting Christians who need to know that God loves them and they don't need to earn it. We are not under the law but under God's wonderful grace, which we don't deserve.

As I was sitting in the church in Whifflet, I was thinking the church needed a change; what it needed was sinners wanting to change. I knew a lot of people in Airdrie and Coatbridge who were struggling with sin. The church needed a good Christian band, some Teen Challenge residents to come and share how they came to know God's Son, Jesus. God showed me a Christian band at the same church in a vision. God had a plan for the people of Coatbridge and Airdrie. He wanted a relationship with them. I had seen many sick people come to know the Lord. God was attracted to these people. I believe it was because they knew their lives weren't right.

I ended up in a flat in between Coatbridge and Airdrie. A good mate of mine, Amy, used to get her Methadone and then come up to my flat. Amy got introduced to heroin at fifteen. She was a good-looking young woman with a good personality. Her ex-boyfriend wasn't too happy about her coming to my flat; he must have thought we were going with each other. Amy knew about me believing in the Bible and about my faith. She didn't believe in God, but I believed God wanted her.

One day I was sitting on my couch, thinking I could start an Overcomers Outreach in my home. I knew a lot of people who were not well, with many different addictions. A lot of them told me they spoke to God in quiet moments, so I decided to go ahead with it. I prayed that it wouldn't happen if it wasn't right for me to do this. Amy and another two men I knew started coming to the meeting every Thursday. I led one of them, Brian, to The Haven when I was going through the Hepatitis C treatment and when I was going through the court case about three years earlier. Another man also went into The Haven at the same time as Brian. I took them to church with me and he received salvation, and Brian said he was already speaking to God. They both walked out of The Haven after a few months.

Overcomers Outreach started off with a few of us and then other people heard about it and started coming too. I could see God using it for His glory. God had given me another chance to help His people. I didn't really preach to people; I was more into telling addicts that they were suffering with an illness, addiction, and God could free them from it. And I would tell them that God loved them. God always wants the people who feel unloved. He wants to be a father to them. And I had to do my bit, to stay away from women.

All was going well, the meetings were being blessed with people, different people every week, Catholics and Protestants, and nearly all of them had problems with drugs or alcohol. That was what I wanted. And on a Sunday, people were turning up for church at Whifflet. I got to tell them all about Teen Challenge, and some were also going to the Teen Challenge bus in Coatbridge and in Whifflet. It was all making a lot more sense. I was seeing God use me, exactly what I wanted. I also needed a deep healing, which only God could do for me. I needed the Holy Spirit to put at ease my past hurts.

I was on a Christian dating site, hoping God would give me a partner and then everything would go smoothly. I met a young woman on the site who was from Trinidad, and she could sing as well. It was like everything I had been praying for was happening. When she came up from London to Scotland to meet me, it fell on the day before my Dad's wedding day. People were at my house at the Overcomers Outreach. I remember a woman called Ruth was there, looking for help with her drug addiction and I told her a bit about Teen Challenge.

My sister, Siobhan drove me to Glasgow Central to meet this woman from the dating site. I saw her walking towards me and she was very attractive. I knew then that God was testing me to see how I dealt with this. I just knew in my spirit she wasn't the partner for me. We met and she was great; she came across as if she liked me. We got back to my flat and talked a bit and then started kissing, but we realized this could end up with us having sex, so I went to my room and she went into the room next to mine. Now I had a choice. Do I obey God or follow the flesh?

Redemption through the blood

The next day she came into my room and we started kissing, and before we knew it we were lying on my bed, still with our clothes on, kissing. All of a sudden the bed broke in the middle and we fell through. I believe God was speaking to us. You see, she was a Christian too. We both had an attraction to each other, but I knew she wasn't going to be my partner. I didn't know how it was going to end up in the future, but God wanted me to do the right thing. I was being tested.

We went to my Dad's wedding that night and my family was saying how beautiful she was. It was great and she looked as though she was enjoying herself. Halfway through the party, she asked if I wanted to go back to my flat and I agreed, so we took a taxi home and I failed the test. It didn't matter how difficult the Christian life was, I still sinned against God's will. I believe that if I had obeyed God's will, He would have blessed me. Remember, I was still not well with the G12 cult I was in. But I knew God had put people in my life and I shouldn't have been making a total mess of it. I became pretty famous to a lot of Christians for this sin.

The next day, the two of us went into Glasgow for a meal. We got back to Airdrie and stopped a taxi, and the driver happened to be my landlord. The woman went back to London the next day, and I was thinking that I had made a mess of it all. God hadn't wanted me to sleep with that woman. It was hard work to say no to a good-looking woman who wanted to sleep with me, but that shouldn't be my excuse, because I knew God had told me not to. Mind, I'm trying to be an example to hurting people. God is very strict on leaders who are not looking after His flock, and that was me. Proverbs ch 26, verse 11: "As a dog returns to its vomit, so a fool repeats his folly."

Things didn't seem the same after that. God wanted me to lead a meeting and I had been disobedient in a sin that God hates. I was called to be a role model to the ones God was calling on. I knew that living as a Christian was harder than I had first thought. God's will isn't always what we want to do. God always makes a way out for you, but you have to follow His ways.

If I had done The Haven program the way it had to be done and allowed God to break me, I wouldn't have had to go through all this. I still had obsessions inside me that God wanted to remove. I had to act on God's promise and believe and be more obedient. That would stop the devil having a foothold in my life. The devil is like a lion ready to devour.

I was on Facebook and I got to know this woman called Angie. She was a Catholic and what she wrote to me about God reminded me of myself. Angie thought Jesus was a Catholic and that He came to earth to start the Catholic religion. That's the way I used to think. I told her a little about myself and how I came to faith and we decided to meet at Glasgow Central. When I met her, I knew it was another test from God. Angie liked me, but I knew I wasn't going to spend my life with her. We went back to my place and my thinking was to have a cup of tea or coffee and then walk her back to the train station. We got back to my flat, sat on the couch and talked, and before we knew it we were kissing. After kissing, we ended up in my room and again I made a mess of things and we slept with each other. In the world, these things might be okay to do. Angie was in the world and didn't see that much wrong with having casual sex, but I had the Holy Spirit in me and I knew God wasn't happy with this lust in my life.

My plan was to repent, but I repented without changing. What I had felt was just remorse. It wasn't repentance. People stopped coming to my meetings, and that was because God didn't want them there. God hates the sin of lust. Soon not one person came to my meetings. Again I repented, but in my heart I did not change.

Angie and I still kept in touch by phone. She wanted a relationship with me, but I knew we weren't meant to be partners. I told her about Roy's cafe where Teen Challenge residents went to share their testimonies about how they came to know Jesus. As she was going there, she actually went to a different church where the leaders also knew me. Angie told them about us going with each other. The leaders in that church knew a worker in The Haven who knew me well. Angie came to stay at my house again and I showed her the Teen Challenge bus in Whifflet and explained the work it did. She loved the bus, so she stayed at my flat and we slept in different rooms. I was thinking that maybe God would bless me now that we didn't go with each other.

New Year came and I decided to go to Davie's, hoping for a blessing from God. We were in Davie and Jean's home for New Year and the worker from The Haven was holding a Bible study, and this was the worker who had heard about me having sex with a woman outside God's will. The worker asked the group if anyone wanted prayer and I put up my hand. Martin, the worker, was happy to see that it was me with my hand up, and we went to another room to pray. Martin knew about the woman I had been with, but he didn't say that God was sorry that I had had such a hard time; he told me God was not pleased with me and I left that room feeling God's wrath over me. I couldn't sleep all that night, as I was experiencing God's conviction of my sins.

The next day, we went to Paisley to a meeting for Christians. The service had started and I saw a picture of Jesus pulling Peter out of the water when Peter was drowning. Jesus' arm was really strong-looking. I felt this conviction, so I went into the toilets, knelt down beside the pan, and started to cry with my eyes shut. All I could see was Jesus' strong arm pulling me out of the water when I was drowning in sin. After it all, I opened my eyes and I felt like a new man. God had forgiven me for my sins. I felt really light and refreshed; it was an amazing time and I couldn't stop smiling.

The night before, Martin had told me that God wanted me to surrender everything. And now God started blessing the Overcomers Outreach meetings again, but still I refused to forgive my enemies and I still wasn't sexually sober.

I met this guy I didn't even know. He needed somewhere to stay, so I told him he could stay at my place. As I went to meet him in a town near Coatbridge, I felt the Holy Spirit inside me saying it was wrong to have him stay with me. It was a strong presence I felt, but instead of believing the Holy Spirit and finding a way out of the situation, I met him and took him home to my flat. I soon realized this guy was going to be hard work. He had no interest in God. After a few weeks, he had to go. He would have walked all over me if he'd stayed any longer. He was the type of man that goes about taking of people and finding ways to use them for himself. No interest in trying to get right before the lord. Lust wasn't my strong area as Christian. I know I made massive mistakes, but I got up, dusted myself down, and aimed for God's kingdom. During the meeting in my flat, my neighbor would always be at my door, complaining about the noise.

I was introduced to Simon, a man in the A.A. recovery program. He was a Roman Catholic who loved the Lord. Simon was also a sex addict, and he attended S.A. (Sexaholics Anonymous). Simon understood a lot about these addictions, and he was like my sponsor.

He had been sexually sober for three months, working through the program a day at a time. He was touched by God as he was confessing his sins to the priest in the confessional box, and after that stopped acting out (masturbating). Simon had been going to A.A. for years, and he could talk the talk at these meetings. One day at A..A, a man who had done the 12 steps correctly was sharing how through it he had got healing on the inside. He said that if we were disturbed by what he was saying, then the disturbance was from within ourselves. Simon told me that he was really angry at this man because he hadn't been off the drink for as long as Simon, but even so this man became Simon's sponsor and he learned to do the 12 steps in the correct way. Simon had already sponsored ten people from A.A. by then, and he had to go back to all of them and apologize, as he hadn't been doing what he was teaching them.

He told me that I shouldn't be holding meetings if I wasn't doing what the word of God was telling me. He told me to forgive my enemies, but there was no way I could do that. So Simon said I would just remain sick. He took me to an A.A. meeting where I met Colin, a guy I had met before. Colin had also done the Teen Challenge program, but after a few good years he had started using again. Then he said to me, with joy in his eyes, that the A.A. was all New Testament work. What the 12 steps teaches is all biblical, but God is a generous God, so people who aren't born again have used the steps, but then I know people who found salvation while doing the 12 steps, and for me at one time got a massive conviction of my sins doing it (it was amazing, God's conviction). Colin had done Teen Challenge and then had worked at The Haven years before he relapsed. He said that he had been full of religion and church and he used to go about saying who was saved and who was not, and he now knew that it was not right to be thinking that way. Peter, my previous sponsor, had also thought when he was a young Christian that God had given him this special power to look into people's eyes and tell if they were born again or not. I believe that is all religious nonsense. I went back home because Simon had some family issues. Then Simon phoned me to say he would have to stop being my sponsor and I lost touch with him.

I carried on, doing the meetings in my flat. Some of my mates who were in addiction still went to the church in Whifflet. One day, one of the leaders of that church asked me to stop bringing my mates to that church because they were either alcoholics or drug addicts, and that church was not qualified to help them. I replied that Jesus hadn't come for the self-righteous but for the sick.

My mate, Paddy got speaking to a man from my area called Greg, and Paddy explained how I was having a hard time in these meetings and needed more help. So Greg turned up one night and was really happy that I had opened up my home for these people. You see, Greg wasn't always a Christian. When he was born again, Greg couldn't believe that God had forgiven him of his sins. That was when Greg was a young man. Whenever I saw Greg, he was always loving sick people just as Jesus had done. That's why the Bible says that those who have been forgiven much also love much. Greg came to the meetings for a few weeks.

One night everyone had left after the meeting except Greg, when my neighbor came round, complaining about the noise as the people had left my flat. Greg suggested that I move the meeting to his church in Coatbridge. I was happy with that and it all went well to begin with. As I was sharing at the meeting, I was honest about my sins of the flesh. People at these meetings are looking for role models, people who are applying God's word to their lives, but I wasn't giving God as much as I should. A few people in the meeting started saying to Greg that it was wrong for me to be holding these meetings when I was not right with God. I was still blaming God for things other Christians had done to me.

After a few months, I had a meeting with Greg, his mate, and also my sponsor, Peter. I had to finish the recovery meeting. At this point, I had a full-time job, and during work I was thinking of going back on drugs. It felt as though the Christian life was just too difficult. I had been off drugs for eight years. A guy I knew from my area told me that the pedophile who abused kids, whose house we had sat in when we were kids, was in jail. Something like twenty years later, the ones who had been abused by him had got together and this was the result. Before this I had been talking with Mark, a mate of mine, about how we had spent a lot of time in that guy's house in our early teens, and how he had seemed to like the company of young kids. I gave up my job and went to stay with my Dad and his wife. I was living in Harthill.

I went to someone's house in Coatbridge and ended up staying with this woman. That night she came in to me with a blue Valium. I could have said, "No thanks," but instead I took it and asked her for a cup of tea (to break it up). The next day I woke up still feeling the effect of the Valium, and I offered to buy more from her, which I took, and left the house out of my face on drugs I just paid for valium. I remember walking away, saying that if the Christian life wasn't for me, then this was the life I wanted back. I loved the feeling of the drugs I took. That drug wasn't enough for me — I wanted heroin.

I went to my two mates, Jazza and Tosh for them to go and buy me it, and they couldn't believe I was back using. They wouldn't buy me any heroin at the start, but eventually I got some and started smoking it. I had bought a few bags. All I can remember is trying to get a hit off them and they wouldn't give me a hit. If they had used a needle on me after I had been clean for over eight years, I believe my body wouldn't have been able to handle it. I woke up the next day looking at the ceiling, not knowing where I was and what had happened the night before. I got a shock. It was like going back to the start after over eight years of hard work. I went back to my Dad's at Harthill, not caring. I still had some Valium on me, enough for only a few days. Roy had heard that I had picked up drugs again and he told me there was a new Teen Challenge that had opened in Leicester, and he suggested I go to do another program. I thought it would be a good chance to get away from all the madness in Scotland, and I saw it as a chance to get a rest. Mind, I had picked up drugs only for a few days. I knew how Teen Challenge worked. I knew Jesus, so it wouldn't be all that difficult. But God had different plans. God was looking inside me and He knew what needed removing. He was planning on doing some serious surgery on me. I was leaving the devil's playground.

TEEN CHALLENGE, LEICESTER

I got off the bus in Nottingham, and one of the staff members was waiting for me to take me to Teen Challenge in Leicester. When I got to the program, it was like a five-star hotel. I went in feeling really confident, put my luggage down in my room, and went downstairs to meet all the guys. It was a Wednesday in July 2013. I was thinking that it would be like a rest for me, away from Scotland and from all temptations. This was going to be great.

The teaching was amazing. In The Haven, I had hated chapel and the classrooms, but this time I wanted to listen. Friday came and we had chapel, and the manager from Teen Challenge was taking it. I couldn't stop crying to God for being so good to me and looking after me. Jay, the manager, came over to me when I was crying, and told me that God was saying that my past was not going to come back on me. I loved it! Sunday came and the service at the first church was based on the same book, chapter and verses that God had spoken from to me before, Genesis ch. 12 vs 1-3.

"The Lord had said to Abraham, "Leave your country, your people and your father's household and go to the land I will show you. I will make you into a great nation and I will bless you: I will make your name great, and you will be a blessing. I will bless those who bless

you, and whoever curses you I will curse; and all peoples on earth will be blessed through you."

Mind, God told me the first thing I needed to do was to kill the giants inside me. That evening, we went to a church in Nottingham and that service was on Romans chapter 8 verse 28, a verse which God had been speaking into my life before I went into Teen Challenge. "And we know that in all things God works for the good of those who love him, who have been called according to his purpose." I knew God was protecting me from the devil's attacks. There were areas inside me that God wanted to remove, as Satan was having a field day with me out there. God had plans for my life, but so did Satan.

It was Monday afternoon and everything was great. After lunch, we went to do our work duties and I was outside doing some sweeping up. As I started my job, I began thinking that I could get a flat somewhere in England and start using drugs. Please believe what I write here. This came from an evil spirit, because the second I started to think about going back to drugs, I felt this heaviness come upon me. It was like I had no more joy. An unclean spirit had attacked me. After I had finished my work, I went back into the center feeling really down. This was when I got attacked with condemnation. I felt I couldn't even breathe with it, as if I was being strangled. Satan had an army and they didn't want me getting well. You could see it in my face that I was struggling, and on these programs there are always those who notice that and start getting cheeky. I didn't want to be there. I hated the place after that experience with the enemy. God was speaking to me about Exodus and the Promised Land that I had been waiting on for a few years. God was telling me that if Moses didn't get to the Promised Land, neither would I unless I killed off the giants inside me.

There were residents at this time rubbing me up the wrong way. One guy I knew from Coatbridge, and he was nearly on Phase Three when I arrived. I had led him to God and got him into The Haven, but he had walked out after a few months. He got full of pride, walking about the program as if he was this ex-hard man, and he was also getting really cheeky with me in front of other people. I was thinking that when I saw him again back in Coatbridge after this program, I'd see if he would still speak to me this way. God was allowing all this stuff to happen to me because He was removing sicknesses in me. God uses people to open you up so God can cut it out of you. It did hurt, but I knew what God was doing in me.

When I was a few weeks into the program, my thinking was that God was going to send me back to Coatbridge to finish the work I had started. One staff member said that God didn't want me back in Scotland, so I ran to my room, picked up my Bible and read Genesis ch 12 vs 1-3, and I noticed something that I hadn't noticed before. It says that God told Abraham to go from his country, his people and his father's household, and go to the land that God would show him. After reading that, I knew God wanted me out of Scotland.

I hadn't been long in the program when I went to a church in Nottingham, and the pastor asked if anyone had been badly hurt by a church and was struggling to forgive, and they were left unwell. If so, then they should come to the front and God would heal them. So I went to the front and God did heal me. After that, Satan didn't give up; he still tried to remind me of it, but I just prayed a blessing over the ones I felt hurt by.

SCHOOL OF MINISTRY

The School of Ministry was teamed up with Teen Challenge, and a lot of ex-residents went there after their program. It gave more teachings into the Bible. It wasn't just for residents who had finished Teen challenge. Residents were doing School of Ministry then getting a job as staff members in Teen challenge. Other residents went on missionary work all around the world. There was a certain woman at the school of ministry who I took a fancy to. She had also finished a women's Teen Challenge Hope House, and she was good looking and it opened me up for God to work on. One night as I was talking to God about her, I looked out of the window and she was speaking to one of the staff members. I started getting angry with God, asking why He was doing this to me. It was messing with my head. The good Lord was using this too to get stuff out of me. I had an obsession for a woman to be my lover (wife).

When Paddy first went into The Haven in February 2006, I was with him and I saw this man who went in with Paddy on the same day. I can remember him staring out of the window, looking lost. He was new to Christian rehabs. He finished The Haven, but didn't change his attitude. When he met a few of his old friends, they asked him how he had got clean off drugs and he had explained that it was rehab, but he was too ashamed to say he had met Jesus. Back in his addiction, he had asked God what He wanted from him and God had replied, "Everything." This man is now a mighty man of God, working in Teen Challenge, Leicester. Brian loves the Lord and Teen Challenge.

COMPASSION

In January that same year, God blessed me through a charity called Compassion, which sponsors children in very poor communities abroad. I chose to sponsor a young girl from Tanzania. I decided to give not only ten percent of my money from Job Seekers (Job Seekers is money for unemployed people looking for work), but I also planned to do a charity walk in Scotland to raise money for the charity. Over the next six months, I went about asking people in Scotland if they would give money to the charity, and I collected one thousand pounds. My Dad and his wife took over sponsoring the girl when I went into Teen Challenge, and I still sponsor the same girl. God has giving me responsibility to provide money for this child and her family. I still sponsor that kid today. It's a total blessing to give to this kid and family in Africa.

A staff member took chapel one morning, and God had given him Isaiah ch 43 verses 18-19 to speak on. "Forget the former things; do not dwell on the past. See, I am doing a new thing! Now it springs up; do you not perceive it? I am making a way in the desert and streams in the wasteland." When he shared it, it really touched my spirit. I could just feel it being from God to my spirit. It was exciting to know God's word being spoken into my life. Do you ever hear God's word and it just connects with your Holy Spirit? Well, that happened to me there.

RENEWAL, BIRMINGHAM

It was the first Tuesday of the month of November. John Carr, the pastor of Renewal Church, asked if anyone wanting prayer would come to the front. As he was speaking I was looking at him, and he pointed at me first and said that everywhere he walked, I was looking at him and no one else was paying as much attention. He added that I had been a Christian for quite a while and God had been drilling me and now I was numb. Then he walked over to another man and told him that if he went back into addiction, he would be dead in three months. That same guy told me that there was a man after him who was getting out of prison in three months. He had been involved in organized crime before he went into Teen challenge. That same guy is doing great today. He went into the School of Ministry.

NOTTINGHAM

I was with Teen Challenge at church and the pastor was speaking from Psalm 89. I was looking through the psalms, trying to find it, when I realized I had folded down one of the corners of the page. As I unfolded it, I could see 89. I knew God was speaking to me again about the Promised Land, and I knew the Promised Land had fields and rivers in it.

A mate from Teen Challenge was going to a place called Horizon. I couldn't remember hearing that much about this place, but before John went there he left me a verse about my Promised Land. It was Deuteronomy ch. 8 verses 6-9.

"Observe the commands of the Lord your God, walking in his ways and revering him. For the Lord your God is bringing you into a good land–a land with streams and pools of water, with springs flowing in the valleys and hills; a land with wheat and barley, vines and fig trees, pomegranates, olive oil and honey; a land where bread will not be scarce and you will lack nothing; a land where the rocks are iron and you can dig copper out of the hills."

December came and then it was New Year, and I was struggling with trying to get over my past, thinking so much into it. The devil was at work, making me feel guilty for the stuff Jesus went to the cross for, taking my punishment. That was what I should have been telling the devil. I gave Satan too much room to get into my life and accuse me of things I had been forgiven for. One of the staff members took me into a room and told me God had given him verses to share with me, verses from Isaiah ch. 43. I replied that they were verses 18-19, and he asked me how I knew that. I told him that God had already spoken about them to me. After that, the Holy Spirit put something like a plug inside me to stop me acting out.

Just before that, I was reading in the gospels about Jesus being baptized in the Jordan River, and God said to me that He would give me a son and I would call him Jordan.

When God was doing this inside work in me, I stopped blaming God. You see, I felt as though my enemies had plenty of blessings like money and material things, and they were sheltered. Even at that, I didn't see God using them to help the sick, or even sick people being attracted to them. There must have been pride in me, saying that I deserved more than them.

At this point, I was sharing a room with a guy I found really hard work. He once told the staff that I had said it was okay to do a program and continue drinking. The staff pulled me in and then he came in and said right in front of me and the staff that I had said that to him. He liked playing silly little games. These are the guys who only act this way in programs, but outside programs, where they don't get away with all that, they treat you with more respect. The roommate I had before him was hard work, too. After I stopped sharing with him, God came into his life and changed him, because the School of Ministry had been praying for him. I left one room and shared with a guy in another room, and this guy was even worse. This was God using them for my benefit. God was cutting things out of me.

January came, and I thought that with some Phase Three guys moving on to the School of Ministry, things would get easier. I didn't think the Phase Three guys were any good for the new residents coming in. I wasn't the only one getting cheek off them. In these programs, you are better off not saying anything sometimes. Teen Challenge wasn't made to be fair; it's how we react to unfair stuff. The purpose of the program is discipleship making, with residents being broken and turned into men and women of God. While all this was going on, every day I was in the chapel, walking in circles, praying. Every chance I had I was in there, praying. I knew that I didn't want to be on the program any longer and only God could keep me there, plus I wanted the Promised Land after I'd finished.

In January, a woman who had just finished at the Hope House women's Teen Challenge came to our program to do the School of Ministry. When I saw her, I thought she was attractive and I couldn't stop thinking about her. I was becoming obsessed. One staff member, a Welsh guy, was a good-looking man, and I thought the two of them liked each other. That made everything so much harder. I remember going outside at night and asking God not to do this to me. I was even thinking of leaving the program, because I had so much of a fancy for her. God was taking stuff out of me at this time. I always had this inside me, always wanting women in my life and thinking everything would then be better once I had them. I was co-dependent. One night I couldn't even sit and eat my dinner, because she was there. I got on Phase Three and I had sixteen weeks left of God doing His work on me, and please believe me, it didn't feel one bit good.

The Welsh guy I mentioned was at one time of his life a very hard man. He used to be the most feared man in the Welsh prisons because he know how to fight. His Dad was the best street fighter in Britain at one time, and there are a few books about his Dad. The son's aim was to be just like his Dad. This same man had a younger brother who went to a Teen Challenge rehab but didn't finish it, but passed the message to his older brother The older brother went in a very angry and damaged man and God just kept breaking him. He was a staff member when I was there. Now that same man is married to a lady that had done Teen Challenge Hope House, and the two of them are living a good and healthy life in the Lord.

I had a few weeks left at Teen Challenge and then I was going to Horizon, the same place John had gone to. I was going there on a Monday. That Sunday night, we were at the same church in Nottingham and the pastor was sharing. He said that there was someone there who had been waiting for the Promised Land for years, like waiting in a queue, and now it was their turn to get served. And I was going to Horizon the next day.

Horizon was in the town of Harrogate. One of the men from the center came with John to pick me up from the town center. The town was absolutely lovely. I got in the van, on my way to my Promised Land eventually. The place was amazing. I couldn't believe how smart it was. It all started with one man who was called by God to set up this center and one woman who offered him match-funding. It was purpose-built for men who had completed Teen Challenge but needed help and training to get a job. I had a meeting with the man who had set up Horizon, and with the chef, and they accepted me. It was Roy who had put me onto this place, and I thought Roy had told them about the charge that put me on the sex offenders list. You see, these places do an enhanced disclosure. The manager at Teen Challenge knew about it, and by the grace of God he had allowed me to stay.

The manager at Horizon got in touch with Teen Challenge not long after my interview, and he said there was no chance I would get in. When I went back to Teen Challenge in Leicester, the manager of Horizon did my disclosure when I left Horizon, and when I was back in Teen Challenge he read on the disclosure that I had been charged with a sexual assault. Even though I had been accepted when I was at Horizon, it changed when the manager read about the charge. My first time at Horizon was an interview. Not long after I heard that, we went to Renewal Church in Birmingham, and as the pastor was about to start the service, he paused and said God was speaking to him about someone there who couldn't get into the Promised Land. He said that when Moses and the Jews got to the Red Sea, God did the impossible and opened up the Red Sea for them to cross. I knew God was speaking to me. When God promises you something, all God wants you to do is trust. I always knew God had plans on this, and now God was telling me to trust and believe.

At this time, I had been accepted for Phase Four in Duns. I wasn't really happy with this, as I had finished the program expecting to go straight into the Promised Land. God had been promising this for years, and I knew God was always looking after me because I was His son. I felt really down, even at the end of the program. I found the program and the work God was doing in me very painful. Duns Teen Challenge was the last place I wanted to go after the program, and that made me even more disappointed. Duns was mostly labor, and I had been expecting to go straight into this great Promised Land God had prepared for me.

I knew the Promised Land was going to be a place with fields and crops. Before I knew about Horizon, I was thinking my Promised Land would be me and my future partner living on a farm, and I imagined my partner galloping about on a white horse. I got to Phase Four and wasn't as excited as I expected, because the Promised Land I was waiting on hadn't come as quickly as I had hoped. That charge was still holding me back, even though I had done my probation and I was not on the sex offenders list, but it still had power over me.

I got to Duns and I wasn't totally happy about it. I really didn't want to be there. I was even thinking about going back on heroin and quitting the Christian life, because I thought it was too difficult. I wanted away from Teen Challenge and a lot of the residents. I honestly just wanted to get on with my life and learn a trade and then get a full-time job. But it seemed the Promised Land was still a far off land. God had removed a lot of stuff from me, and at this time I felt really worn out with the program. After about six weeks, I got fed up with Duns and decided to go back to Scotland. It seemed like I was going even farther away from the Promised Land.

I went to my Dad's in Harthill. My Dad had medication in the house and I knew where it was. In 2004, after I had been eight weeks in The Haven, I got out to visit my family. As I was returning, back to The Haven, my Dad took a heart attack. He needed a triple bypass and it left him with some brain damage. The medication he was on was Valium, a drug I enjoyed. I went to the kitchen drawer and took some. After that, I became an addict again. I'm an all-or-nothing sort of guy. Not long after that, I went back on heroin and even started drinking alcohol again.

I knew the Promised Land was getting even farther away now. I began to do everything the flesh desired. I was back injecting the drug, but however much drugs I took, there was still this little voice saying that I wasn't called to be an addict; I was God's child; my body was the Lord's temple. When my family found out, they weren't that surprised. I felt really disappointed with Teen Challenge, because only two staff members kept in touch with me, and when I told them I was back on drugs they never contacted me again. It was like there was no support out there for Teen Challenge ex-residents. Church wasn't giving me much help. In fact, all I was feeling was guilt if I went to church, so I lost interest. When you know your salvation and you are back in the darkness, it's never the same. The Bible says that when you go back to your old sinful life, the demons that come in will be worse than at first.

I was buying drugs and using with people I used to take to church, telling them how much Jesus loved them and that they didn't have to live that way. And there I was, using drugs again with them. I remember smoking dope and honestly freaking right out, thinking that certain men were going to get me. Paranoia again came in very quickly; it seemed so real at the time.

F.E.A.R. **F**alse **E**vidence **A**ppearing **R**eal... It was like I was just waiting for something really bad to happen to me. I wasn't even that long back in addiction and all its sicknesses came back into my life. For those who know the Lord and fall back into sin, the cross is still waiting on you.

Jane phoned me to see if I could help her older sister. Now I had met Jane at A.A., and she had also come along to the Overcomers' Outreach I was doing. One night, Jane met me in her car and I told her I had some drugs, not knowing that she had been off all drugs for a few months since she had been going to church, and she was doing well. She asked if she could have some of my drugs. I looked at her; she looked different in a good way. Then both of us took drugs that night and we went back to her place. I had started using heroin again, but Jane didn't take any of that; plus she had a child and I didn't want to bring all my baggage into their lives. Jane was okay with me being there, but I wasn't. I was paranoid and kept thinking someone she knew would turn up at her home and not be happy to find me there. Jane had a good heart and was doing a great job bringing up her child. I was with Jane for two to three months and treated her child as I would have treated my own.

I attended a Christian meeting in Airdrie where a woman prayed for me. God touched me and I know and felt God was telling me to give up drugs and He would take me to the Promised Land in His time. I went back to Jane's and told her what had happened, but instead of putting all my drugs in the bin straight away, I smoked two joints first, and started to stay clean from addiction the next day. Jane and I were still living together in sin, but off the drugs. I prayed about this a lot, but felt I should stay with her. God was still at work in my life and not convicting me of having sex outside marriage, even though both of us knew it was wrong. When we went to church, we felt guilty about the way we were living.

After a few months, Jane offered me some Valium and I took it, even though I knew I shouldn't. One drug isn't enough for me. The minute I took one, I would start wanting more. Not long after that, I left Jane's home with the plan of meeting up with Big James and getting heroin, even though I had been off heroin for a few months. Big James made a phone call for the drug and we set off to collect it from the dealer. I paid for it, and as we walked back to his house, I asked if he had any clean syringes, as I was thinking of injecting it. Then Jane phoned, saying she knew I was going to buy some heroin, but I denied it. Jane went on to say she knew I was buying some and that I had better not inject it. I admitted to Jane she was right and I had got heroin, but I wouldn't inject it. Jane went on to say that God had told her to phone me and tell me not to inject the heroin. I believe my body wouldn't have been able to handle the injecting and I would have overdosed. Remember, I had been clean from it for a few months.

Every time I used drugs, I felt as though I was getting further away from the will of God. Some days later, I went back to Jane's and knew I had made a mistake. I knew God didn't want me using drugs, and if I continued in this sin, I would never get to live in the land God had promised me. One night I left Jane's to help on the Teen Challenge bus in Coatbridge (Whifflet) and guess who walked in — it was the guy I had led to Jesus and had got into The Haven. In these programs, as I mentioned before, a lot of residents rub you up the wrong way, but they wouldn't do this outside the program. He walked out of The Haven, but did Teen Challenge with me. I wanted to see if he was still this hard man, so as he came on the bus, I asked him to come outside with me so I could talk with him. He knew why I wanted to talk with him and we went off the bus and spoke together, not aggressively. Back on the bus, I sat down, and as he was walking towards me I gave him a bit of a look. He turned around and walked off the bus, got into his car, and drove away.

FEBRUARY 2014

I went to King's Church in Coatbridge one Monday, and there were only a few of us in the meeting. Someone read out loud Deuteronomy ch 8 verses 7-9: "For the Lord your God is bringing you into a good land — a land with streams and pools of water, with springs flowing in the valleys and hills; a land with wheat and barley, vines and fig trees, pomegranates, olive oil and honey; a land where bread will not be scarce and you will lack nothing; a land where the rocks are iron and you can dig copper out of the hills." These were the same verses that were given to me in Teen Challenge, about the Promised Land. It was like God was putting a little seed in me about moving me out of Scotland.

I met Jane in Airdrie and she was in a bad mood with me about something so silly. We went into a cafe and ordered two coffees, and then Jane got really angry and threw the cup across the room. I walked out, saying she was a nutcase. (I had moved her out of the way to let someone else pass and I think she had got the wrong idea.) So I thought I'd go off to get some drugs and I went to Big James' to get heroin and Valium. I sat in his house, smoking heroin and taking Valium, and left later that night and headed down to my Mum's, totally out of my face. I had no peace, however much drugs

I took. The Holy Spirit was telling me this wasn't the person God had made me to be. I could feel the Holy Spirit inside me giving me no rest with the drugs, a strong presence of my salvation.

The next day, I still had a small box of Valium on me and I wanted to get help from somewhere, because I knew what the Lord wanted from me and I had to be clean from drugs to do God's will. I picked up my mobile phone, and for some reason decided to phone Sean, my Aunt Jean's ex-boyfriend, the one who had led me to Jesus. I phoned his number and guess what — he just happened to be driving past my Mum's house. I spoke to Sean for about a minute, and before I knew it he was outside the flat. Sean took the drugs and got rid of them. Now I knew God was looking after me again.

Not long after that, as I was walking through Airdrie, I was looking through my wallet and I came across the Horizon card and phone number. This was the place God was calling my Promised Land. I phoned up to speak to the manager, and he said I could go to Horizon that week. I told Jane and she seemed fine with it, and I thought that Jane and her child could come, we could get married and then everything would go well. In addition, I would be working full-time after I finished at Horizon. I knew I was going to the land I had been waiting years for and I was getting away from all the madness of my life in Scotland. There was another chapter happening in my life.

I didn't really know what to expect, but my life was always like that anyway. I always took chances, but this time God was in charge. If it hadn't been for Horizon allowing me in, I would never have survived out there. I was struggling with sin and I was fed up with the Christian life, as I believed it was too difficult, even though God had done some amazing work in me. Horizon was like a safety net for me and it was the work of Christ that gave me this gift. When God spoke to me in Deuteronomy ch.8, vs.7-9, I needed to read to the end of that chapter, verse 19: *"If you ever forget the Lord your God and follow other gods and worship and bow down to them, I testify against you today that you will surely be destroyed."* That verse stuck in my heart, and when God spoke of false gods, for me that meant drugs. It was as if God was saying that if I kept going back to addiction, He wouldn't always be there to protect me. If I went back to my previous lifestyle in darkness, I wouldn't survive it.

HORIZON

I stayed at my Mum's the night before I set off for Horizon, the place I had been waiting years to get to. God had done a lot of work in me before this day. I never understood why God had been preparing me for so long, and why He hadn't just taken me to the Promised Land earlier. I caught the train to Glasgow early in the morning, and from there I took the bus to Harrogate, arriving in the evening. The manager and a few of the guys from the center were there to pick me up and take me to Horizon. It was an amazing place. I had my own room with toilet and shower. I loved it! I was told that this was not a program, and the next day I was given a welcome sheet with a particular verse for each resident. The staff chose a different verse for each resident and guess what mine was — the same verse that God had been speaking to me for years, Romans ch.8 verse 28: *"And we know that in all things God works for the good of those who love him, who have been called according to his purpose."* God was reminding me that I was at last where He wanted me to be.

There were some guys there who had only done a few months in Teen Challenge and had then left without completing the program. These guys were still broken and not put back together again by God. The manager took these guys in and I could see they needed help. I wanted to work as a chef and learn kitchen skills, but I hadn't realized how difficult that job was.

Horizon Life was an absolute blessing from God. It was in a lovely part of England and they seemed like hard-working people. I came to this place to do the will of God and also to get full-time work.

Once again I felt that one of the staff was picking on me, pushing my buttons, and that other residents were more favored. For me, it was a bit like being back on a program. It was like this staff member didn't want me there, but Jesus wanted me to grow there. I felt as if I was being walked all over. I knew how to throw a punch, but I couldn't hit this man because I was aiming to do what God was saying to me, so I left it to God to sort out. But I was angry about this. Remember, I had waited years on this and now I was here I found there was one man who was making life difficult for me. Bit by bit, I was getting drained with it all and fed up with the Christians, and I started wanting to go back to my old life again.

After about six weeks into my stay there, when I was feeling really down with it all, one of the workers there came up to me and told me that God had a message for me. He read verses from 2 Timothy ch 2, verses 20 and 21: *"In a large house there are articles not only of gold and silver, but also of wood and clay; some are for noble purposes and some for ignoble. If a man cleanses himself from the latter, he will be an instrument for noble purposes, made holy, useful to the Master and prepared to do any good work."*

I knew then that God wanted me to be sexually clean. This had happened to me before, but I had always gone back to acting out and watching porn. It was one area of being a Christian that always got me a bad name, and other Christians judged me for it. Now I knew

God wanted to make this area of weakness into an area of strength, so God could get the glory.

This same man of God again had a message for me, and it was that I should finish with Jane. I didn't want to hear that, but I knew it was from God. I missed Jane's child as much as anything, because I had been like a dad to the kid. The two of us finished, but we kept in contact even though I had been told not to, and to hand them both over to God. I didn't exactly do that. I still kept a little bit to myself, and that was still speaking to her on the phone.

I was trying to learn the work I was given in the kitchen, but my concentration wasn't too good. In the mornings I would get up early and go into the kitchen to make the sandwiches for the guys doing landscaping, and I honestly found that difficult as every one of the guys wanted different sandwiches. I had one hour to get it done, and even that stressed me out.

SCOTLAND FOR GRADUATION

A group of us went back to The Haven in Kilmacolm for the graduation. One of our guys was getting his certificate for completing the program there, and another one was speaking at the ceremony. He happened to be an ex-Teen Challenge graduate and he spoke on Deuteronomy chapter 30. I opened my Bible at that chapter and verse and the first thing I saw was the name Jordan. God had spoken to me in Teen Challenge, Leicester, about when I crossed my Jordan River I had to call my son Jordan. There is also a river behind Horizon. The verses that pierced my heart were Deuteronomy ch. 30, verses 17–18: *"But if your heart turns away and you are not obedient, and if you are drawn away to bow down to other gods and worship them, I declare to you this day that you will certainly be destroyed. You will not live long in the land you are crossing the Jordan to enter and possess."*

After reading that, I knew God was saying to me that if I continued in drug addiction I would be dead. He was clearly saying that I wouldn't survive in the world without Him.

I was moved from the kitchen into making coffee in a coffee van that had been bought by Horizon. I could see myself selling coffees one day and selling Christian books, if that was in the will of God.

The whole vision of building Horizon as a center for training in life skills had cost two million pounds. As I said before, this place was a gift from our Savior, Jesus Christ. It was brilliantly equipped and was amazing. There were some very good teachers there too. Another vision from God was to start a women's center for those women who had finished their program at Hope House women's Teen Challenge. A pub had been bought and was being turned into a coffee shop as a place for them to live and work. The people running these two charities were very hard-working. They would do anything they could to get full-time work for the residents. The manager was a hands-on Christian who loved to bring people to salvation, and his wife was an absolutely lovely, caring woman who loved every single one of us.

The center did a Teen Challenge outreach in the city of Leeds, in an area really lacking the love of Jesus Christ. It was a Muslim area, but a lot of them respected our faith, and one of them allowed us to pray with him. I found that the reaction to us in England was different from in Scotland. I had done outreach work in Scotland near enough every week and we spoke more about Teen Challenge than about the Bible. In Scotland, it seemed more about religion than anything, and the people just wanted to be off drugs and drink, and didn't want it to be too religious. I could understand that.

It was November 2014, and I had spent over eight months at Horizon, but I couldn't get on with the manager, so I looked to move on. There was a couple in Leeds I had gotten to know, and they had a love for Teen Challenge and the residents. I met them on a Sunday and they agreed that I could stay with them from that Wednesday. I couldn't wait those two days. I wanted out, so on the Monday I went to a hotel in Leeds. I had a laptop on me. For six-and-a-half months before buying the laptop I had been clean from any acting out or porn. I had got the laptop for practicing my theory driving test, but still when I bought it I knew that there was a part of me that wanted to watch porn, and that was on my mind when I got to the hotel. I knew that this sin had always had a massive grip on my life. When things weren't going well and I felt really down, I would do what addicts do and that's to turn to their addictions to make them feel better. Feeding the flesh felt like the thing I wanted most. This sin off sex always got me a bad name, especially when I became a Christian. God always pointed at this area for me to surrender. When I got to the hotel room I watched porn and acted out after doing so well away from this sin.

Even today God still wants me to give my whole body to Him. It's not easy. Even now I tell myself that if I do what God says, I will get the benefits of it, so why don't I just trust God more? Psalm 37 verses 23 and 24 says, *"If the Lord delights in a man's way, he makes his steps firm; though he stumbles he will not fall, for the Lord upholds him with his hand."* I spent years blaming God for the ways Christians treated me. After the second Teen Challenge program, God took all that out of me. I never blamed God after that.

I was welcomed into the couple's house in Leeds on the Wednesday, knowing that this wouldn't be where God wanted me to be long-term. I did feel pretty disappointed about where I was and the way I felt I had been treated at Horizon, but I had done what God had told me, and that was to praise Him even when things weren't going too well. I still wanted to quit the Christian life and feed the flesh, but I knew that God had warned me, and that He wanted this book written. I wanted to fulfil my purpose. I knew there was more than this. I was aware there was a lot of opportunity for sin in Leeds and I knew where to find it, but God was saying to me it was not worth it compared to what He had for me.

I still kept in touch with Jane, even though I knew I should just leave that in God's care and close the door on it. I started going to a church there where nearly everyone was black. "I bet there are really good singers in this church," I thought as I went in, and do you know what? I was right! This church knew how to worship. They seemed madly in love with Jesus and so grateful for the cross.

During this time, Jane was hanging around with some of my old mates in Coatbridge and, of course, I wasn't too happy with that. All sorts of things were going on in my head. I decided to go back to Scotland just before New Year and visit Jane and her kid. I knew it was a bad idea. So I got the train to Glasgow where Jane was meeting me, and if I'm honest with myself, I knew I would go back to her house after New Year and I would end up staying, and it's pointless writing about what would happen next. I got off the train and Jane and her kid were there to welcome me. The first thing I noticed was that she looked different, healthier. The three of us left the train station and went to find Jane's car.

The second we got into the car, I knew that what I was planning to do wasn't in the will of God. As we got back to Jane's home and she put her kid to bed, I was thinking that since I was going to sin against God anyway, I might as well use drugs as well. I asked Jane for Temazepam and Valium, and do you know what? I eventually found them. As I was taking them, I remembered what God had told me in Deuteronomy ch. 8 and ch. 30, that I would be destroyed if I went back to worshipping false gods, but I still took them. I was also thinking of my family's salvation.

I can hardly remember anything after that, because I had made myself a cup of coffee to break down the drugs so they would have a quicker effect. It doesn't take a lot of hard work to become an addict again, just one bad decision. The next day, Jane and I drove into Coatbridge to meet someone Jane knew. When we walked into their kitchen, her friend had three lines of cocaine waiting for us. The two of us weren't expecting this. I took the piece of paper, put it up my nose and went for the biggest and fattest line of coke. Then after that I just kept buying more, and again I could hardly remember anything, as I had done so much cocaine. The next day came and the only thing on my mind was heroin. People seem to think cocaine is a cool drug and heroin is a dirty drug, but I know that's not true.

I left Jane's home thinking I would go and get certain mates, then get some heroin to share together and find a safe home to take it in, as I didn't want to inject it too soon. I called at the house of a mate who used to come to church with me, and sometimes his partner would come too. I got the heroin I wanted and smoked it to bring me down from the previous night's cocaine. This mate I was using heroin with had at one point wanted to join a Teen Challenge program. He used to go to the Teen Challenge bus with me as well. And here I was, using with him and his partner again.

I left their home and headed back up to Jane's. I could still feel the cocaine from the night before, and I was now using the heroin to stop me feeling so low from that. The next day, Monday, I had to leave Jane's to get more heroin. You see, Jane hated the drug heroin and she hated me taking it, but all I cared about was myself — the mind of a drug addict all over again. I got the drug I wanted off another mate who went to church with me. This same guy had been touched by the Holy Spirit before I became a Christian. I got one bag off him and I snorted it up my nose, again got a coffee, and then as that wasn't enough, I met him again and bought another bag off him. But this time I wanted to inject it. I went into a chemist to get clean syringes, and then I knew which house to go to.

I was good friends with this family from Sikeside and Greenend, and two of the brothers had also gone to church with me. There had been three brothers, but now two of them were dead due to excessive alcohol. The third brother still had the home in Greened. I knew the house and I knew the people who met in this house would be drinkers, but a lot of crazy things had happened in this house through violence, alcohol, and violent behavior. When I arrived, everything seemed fine, and I knew almost everyone there. Just one guy was new to me. I asked my mate if I could go into the toilet for a while, and he knew what I meant. I went into the toilet, got out my needles and other stuff and injected half the bag, as I wasn't sure if I would overdose if I took more.

I went back into the living room and offered to get some alcohol from the shops for any who wanted some. When I returned with the drinks, the one man I didn't know was standing up, shouting about me hitting up heroin in the toilet. This guy didn't like heroin addicts. I gave the people in the house their drinks, sat down and this guy turned around and said that he remembered me and didn't like me. He was pretty well built and tall, and I didn't want any trouble. I still had that other half of the heroin, so I went into the toilet to finish it before this guy started getting aggressive towards me. He seemed like the type of man who, if he didn't beat you in a fight, would go into the kitchen to get a knife and stab you without thinking twice. As I was taking the rest of the drug, the toilet door opened and Big Skin was there, a friend from Sikeside. The other man was still going

Redemption through the blood

on about me hitting up heroin in the toilet, and the rest were trying to calm him down. I sat down and asked another person there if I could roll him a joint. He gave me his tin of tobacco with a lump of dope in it; I rolled the joint and gave it to the mad man. He smoked it, it knocked him out and I left the house.

When I left the house, it was as if God was saying that my chances were up; no more rounds. Next time I was down, I would be staying down. I went to my Mum's flat and went straight to bed, as I didn't want her to know I was back on drugs. But my Mum knew. I woke up the next day not feeling too good and still withdrawing from the drugs, mostly the cocaine. I had money in the bank and I could have gone out and got drugs, but all I wanted was the next day to come so I could head back to England and get a fresh start.

I got up the next morning and couldn't wait to get out of Scotland, repent, and start all over again. I got back to the home I was staying in in Leeds, got the book I had started and put it in the bin, and started this book all over again. It took four weeks before all the drugs had left my system, and eventually I felt my confidence coming back. It's hard coming off cocaine, as it can make you feel suicidal. I began working as a volunteer in a cafe in Leeds, thanks to the man who I was staying with. It was the start of January 2015. I knew God had told me to stay close to Him because He wanted His will done in my life. I still struggled with certain areas of the flesh at this time. I was living and working in a city, and it was so easy to get sidetracked away. All I ever wanted to do was to surrender my body to the Lord. It wasn't like I didn't care about pleasing Jesus with my body, because I did care. It was an every day choice I had to make. I had my good days and my not so good days, but God was always the same to me. Two months later, in March, I managed to get my own flat from the church where I was attending. I needed my own space, but I also knew that somehow God was going to take me back to Horizon.

After work one day, I noticed a man in the street with a sign over him, with writing about salvation through the cross of Jesus. I asked him what his opinion was about salvation, and he told me that when you are born again (or saved), you cannot lose your salvation because it is sealed. Then I asked the other Christian man with him the same question and this man disagreed, asking me how I knew my name was written in the book of life in heaven. I said I had been born again. He replied that if God could remove my name, why would He put it in? After that, I decided I had heard enough. I walked away from that and had learned one thing: that some Christians believe you can lose your salvation and some believe you cannot. I had to work out for myself how I understood what God was saying.

God had used uncomfortable characters in my life to teach me to keep my mouth shut, because God was cutting out areas of my life that He didn't want me to have. It was painful, inside work the Lord had to do in me. I was honoring God no matter how unfair life seemed to be. One good thing about having enemies is that it kept me on my toes and I could see the Lord working on it instead of doing it my way. When I get tested by certain people, it allows me to look at my own heart and see what's in it.

I started getting the feeling that God wanted me back at Horizon sooner than I thought. I had been away from there for five months. I had to go back to Harrogate as I had an appointment to see my doctor. I got off the bus in Harrogate and spoke to God and said, "You want me back here, Father." After the appointment, I was walking to the bus stop to return to Leeds when I noticed the Horizon manager driving past. He stopped, turned the car round, drove up to me and told me to jump in. So I did, knowing it was from God. He asked if I would like to come back into Horizon and I said yes, as I was waiting on God to take me back there. This was on 15th April, 2015, and I was back in Horizon by 22nd April, just a week later.

POST SCRIPT

Currently, Paul is living with a friend from another church and is working full time in a restaurant in Harrogate as a K.P., Kitchen Porter. It's called Farm Whole Foods And Bistro. He honestly loves his job, as the ones he is working with are all so friendly and the manager and his wife and kids all treat them great. They are building a family with the staff.

Paul hopes all who read his story will find God to be as faithful to them as God has proved over and over again to Paul.

GLOSSARY

Chip pan..........................Pan for cooking fries
Orange walks.....................annual marches of the Orange Order (N.I. Protestants)
Hibs walks.......................annual marches of the Hibernians (N.I. Roman Catholics)
N.I..............................Northern Irish
Red Ash path.....................weatherproof gravel and cinder path
stooky...........................plaster cast for broken limb